Iceland Travel Guide

2023

The Ultimate Travel Guide For Planning Your Trip To Iceland From Where to Visit, What To Do And When To Visit, Everything You Need To Know.

Jon Fridrik and Evelyn Noah

Table of Contents

CHAPTER 1

History of Iceland

Iceland is a nation of islands in the North Atlantic. Iceland is a country of striking climatic, geographic, and cultural differences because it is located on the continuously moving tectonic boundary between Europe and North America. Sparkling glaciers, including Europe's largest Vatna Glacier (Vatnajökull), cover its craggy mountain ranges; some numbers of hot geysers heat many of the nation's buildings and homes and enable year-round hothouse farming, and the offshore Gulf Stream maintains a surprisingly mild climate for one of the world's most northerly inhabited regions.

Over a thousand years ago, during the Viking era of discovery, a community of mixed Norse and Celtic people established Iceland. The first community, mostly made up of Norwegian seamen and explorers, encouraged additional forays to Greenland and the North American coast (which the Norse called Vinland). Despite being geographically separated from Scotland, its nearest European neighbor, by about 500 miles (800 km), Iceland has remained an integral component of

European civilization throughout its history. The Icelandic sagas are regarded as among the finest literary achievements of the Middle Ages, reflecting a European outlook while honoring the history and customs of a people far removed from continental centers of commerce and culture. The majority of the sagas recount heroic episodes that occurred during the time the island was settled.

10 Incredible Locations To Check Off Your Bucket List.

For ages, adventurous travelers have been drawn to the Land of Fire and Ice. Ancient lava fields, glittering glaciers, obsidian beaches, diamond icebergs, soaring mountains, and gushing waterfalls have all been carved out of its terrain.

The greatest sites to visit in Iceland are listed here if you're thinking about traveling to this amazing nation. We've included both well-known attractions and some undiscovered treasures in our list. So, if you're looking for advice on how to cross items off your bucket list while visiting Iceland, look no further.

REYKJAVIK

Reykjavik is where most vacations to Iceland begin, but it's hardly a one-stop shop. An excellent method to learn about the nation and its culture is to begin or conclude your trip to the capital.

You may discover exquisite restaurants, upscale shopping, and hip pubs in Reykjavik. However, its well-known sites, museums, and cultural attractions are where its true beauty lies.

Admire Hallgrimskirkja.

Start by going to Hallgrmskirkja, a famous church in Reykjavik whose design was influenced by the surrounding volcanic scenery. This is Iceland's biggest church, rising 73 meters high! To gain a panoramic perspective of the city below, you may even take an elevator up the tower!

The statue of Leif Eriksson, a renowned explorer who is said to have been the first European to set foot in North America sometime about the year 1000, is located in front.

Harpa Concert Hall hosts performances.

Another notable building in the city is the Harpa Concert Hall, which also acts as a cultural center by hosting several musical events and festivals. You may enjoy operatic renditions of Viking sagas, symphony orchestras, jazz festivals, and modern bands whenever you visit Reykjavik.

Check out the Perlan Museum.

Visit Perlan Museum while you're in the city whether or not you plan to travel the country to see its rocky and stunning landscapes, sculpted by both fire and ice.

Highlighting Iceland's natural beauty is the main objective of this interactive exhibit. It is the ideal setting for learning and experiencing everything in one spot.

This also means that when you're there, you'll be treated to an excellent perspective of the city because Perlan is perched atop Skjuhl Hill. This is a great way to begin a tour of the countryside of Iceland.

BLUE LAGOON

The renowned Blue Lagoon is located on the Reykjanes peninsula in southwest Iceland. One of Iceland's top tourist destinations, the Blue Lagoon is featured in both Instagram pictures and advertising campaigns. And we can assure you that the attention is merited.

The Blue Lagoon is a geothermal spa, which means the water is heated to a comfortable 39°C (102°F) by the adjacent geothermal plant. The milky water appears ethereal in contrast to the black lava desert backdrop. It is a real must-see since it is so serene, lovely, and famous.

It is the perfect addition to your trip, either at the start or the finish of your Icelandic excursions, due to its proximity to the airport and its proximity to Reykjavik.

GOLDEN CIRCLE

The Golden Circle should be on your road trip itinerary at least once in your lifetime, whether you elect to self-drive or sign up for a guided group tour. The historical core of Iceland and some of its most breathtaking (and well-known) natural attractions, including towering waterfalls, geysers, and hot springs, are all located in this area.

Visit Thingvellir National Park to be inspired.

The Thingvellir National Park is an important heritage site, in part due to its physical significance (it is located at the meeting point of the tectonic plates of Eurasia and North America), and in part due to its significance in Icelandic history. Here, in the year 930, more than 30 of Iceland's reigning chiefs gathered to form a basic form of representative government. The ruins of that location may still be seen today as you stroll through this breathtaking environment.

Geysir and Strokkur will raise the temperature

Iceland is renowned for both its hot springs and geothermal energy. The enormous Geysir hot spring is arguably the most well-known. When active, this geyser sprays water up to a height of 70m into the air (active periods can last for years) (230 feet). The far more dependable Strokkur geyser is close by. It may reach heights of up to 40 meters and erupts every 5 to 10 minutes (130 feet).

Go for a walk along Gullfoss' brink.

Golden Falls, which is translated as "Gullfoss" in the Icelandic language, is a stunning waterfall that is best seen in the daylight. The glacier Langjökull's ice tunnels, which flow to the Hvtá River, feed the falls, which are a magnificent way to become acquainted with Iceland's waterfalls.

GLACIER LAGOON OF JÖKULSÁRLÓN

Without seeing some ice, what good is a trip to Iceland? A glacial lagoon known as Jökulsárlón is home to icebergs that are brilliant white and electric blue.

Observe them as they float out to sea and over the lagoon. Some even wash ashore to adorn Breiamerkursandur's shoreline, which is now famously known as Diamond Beach. This is the spot for photographers, explorers, and romantics.

SELJALANDSFOSS

You'll quickly learn why you need to see so many waterfalls when traveling Iceland since each one is distinctive and alluring in its own way.

Seljalandsfoss, one of the most popular waterfalls in the nation, is a place you must see (after Gulfoss in the Golden Circle). This waterfall is located on the Seljalandsá River, which originates at the well-known volcano Eyjafjallajökull with its glacier-topped summit.

Its distinguishing feature is the cliff's form, which enables guests to stroll behind the water's curtain.

At the base of the falls, there is a trail, however, you should use caution because it might be hazardous.

Another beautiful waterfall nearby is Gljfrabi, which is hidden within a small canyon. It is definitely a hidden gem, and for amazing photographs, it could be worth the extra effort.

You may also make a stop at Skógafoss, a spectacular waterfall with a 60-meter height, which is 30 minutes away by car. According to mythology, the first Viking settlement in the region concealed a treasure in the cave below the waterfall.

LAKE MYVATN

The fourth-largest lake in Iceland, Lake myvatn, is located in the north and has an otherworldly landscape since it is surrounded by active volcanoes. Beyond the fact that this was the location for the production of several blockbuster movies, including Game of Thrones, this area is home to a staggering number of unique flora and animals (ideal for keen bird watchers).

On a tour around the Diamond Circle, you may discover Lake myvatn and the surrounding area.

Take a bath in the Myvatn Nature Baths.

Make sure to visit the Myvatn Nature Baths if you've been traveling for a few days and would want to unwind in geothermal water. In fact, they are regarded as the Blue Lagoon of the north.

Impress yourself with Krafla and Viti crater.

It's time for fire now that you've experienced ice! Make sure to stop at Krafla, a 10-kilometer-long crater located close to Lake Myvatn (7 miles).

It is a still-active collapsing volcanic region where you can also discover the Viti explosive crater. Viti crater, which translates to "Crater of Hell," is currently a lake with a deep turquoise hue.

This land's moon-like scenery is unlike anything you've ever seen, having been shaped and remade by the volcanic terrain.

AKUREYRI

The second biggest city in Iceland is this charming
holdfast in the north. This "Capital of the North"
offers a wide variety of activities and is located at
the foot of Eyjafjörur Fjord.

Look around the city.

As you stroll the streets, take in the city's landmark
cathedral, the Akureyri Botanical Gardens, and the
Laufas Turf Dwellings, which are cute, turf-topped
illustrations of how Icelandic homes were
constructed in the past.

Observe whales

Discovering the local flora is one of the best things you can do when you're in the north.

You may ride Iceland's gentle and hardy horses across the area's spectacular environment.

If you wish to see some humpback whales, this is also a fantastic location for a whale-watching boat tour around the Tröllaskagi (Troll Peninsula).

VÍK

The settlement of Vik, which is tucked next to seashore cliffs and faces the powerful Atlantic Ocean, is located on the south coast. This little town, which is situated directly by the Myrdalsjökull Glacier, offers a genuine glimpse into coastal life in Iceland. The Arctic tern and puffin populations that have settled in this region of the nation will delight wildlife aficionados.

The rock formations of Dyrhólaey and Reynisdrangar have contributed to Vik's growing popularity as a resting place. The first relates to a peninsula that terminates in a jumping black lava arch, and the second is an allusion to the amazing volcanic sea stacks that form the intimidating cliffs. What a sight this is!

Investigate the northern lights.

This area is one of many fantastic locations where you may try to see the northern lights due to the tiny population of Vik and the low local light pollution. Being a natural occurrence, observations of the aurora borealis cannot be guaranteed, although the greatest time of year to observe it is in the winter.

SNAEFELLSNES

Iceland has a Wild West feel to it too! West Iceland is a remote area that will be worthwhile for the trip!

The Snaefellsnes Peninsula is a tiny version of Iceland and is renowned for its spectacular vistas. This 90-km-long peninsula, which includes lava fields, craters, waterfalls, hot springs, basalt columns, gorges, volcanoes, and charming fishing villages, will demonstrate the variety of the Icelandic landscape.

The 1446-meter-tall Snaefellsjökull stratovolcano and its brilliant glacier, which dominate the landscape, are the namesake of Iceland's oldest national park, Snaefellsjökull.

THE NATIONAL PARK AT VATNAJÖKULL

We travel to Vatnajökull National Park, the largest in Europe, from Snaefellsnes, the smallest national park in Iceland.

In the Highlands, you might feel high.

Iceland's central highlands are where Vatnajökull extends. The country's namesakes, fire and ice, have sculpted magnificent gorges, glacial rivers, and volcanoes that make up the highlands. This is the place to go if you want to view mountains and the breathtaking Svartifoss waterfall.

See the greatest glacier in Iceland!

The Vatnajökull glacier, which dominates the park and has been chiseling its way through the Highlands for thousands of years, must be visited if you visit this magnificent natural reserve.

It is also the biggest glacier in all of Europe. It encompasses 8000 km2, or 8% of Iceland's landmass, while the park itself occupies 14% of that area.

Make sure to check any of them off your bucket list if you visit Iceland.

CHAPTER 2

Places and Locations To Stay On Your Vacation

If you're seeking the greatest locations to stay in Iceland, you could find out all of a sudden that you've won the lottery. There is always something amazing around, whether it be delicious food, imposing and rocky alpine vistas, roaring waterfalls, or quaint fishing villages, no matter where you are in the nation.

Iceland has been a popular tourist destination in recent years because of inexpensive airfare and free layovers between the US and Europe. Towns are few in Iceland, though, and tourists on a tight budget who are drawn there by cheap airfares could be dismayed by the country's exorbitant food and lodging costs. However, due to the popularity of the nation, there are many different types of Iceland hotels available for travelers on a budget as well as those seeking a little bit of luxury. Once you are aware of your alternatives, choosing a place to stay in Iceland is a lot simpler than you may imagine!

If you're searching for somewhere to stay in Iceland other than the main city of Reykjavik, you should plan well in advance due to the busy tourist seasons and small fishing communities. Iceland offers a wide variety of unusual lodging options close to its varied landscape, hot springs, waterfalls, beaches, glaciers, national parks, wildlife, and other attractions. Don't pass up this opportunity! And if you're on a tight budget, you may also locate cheaper Iceland lodgings nearer to the major towns and cities.

The entire year is a great time to visit Iceland. Therefore, it doesn't matter if you're looking for places to stay in Iceland during the winter or the summer. The greatest lodging options in Iceland are suitable for all seasons.

Plan your Icelandic vacation.
Avoid hidden costs in the currency rate while using the Wise Card to withdraw money from one of the many millions of ATMs located across the world, make purchases in stores and restaurants, and pay for your lodging and travel. With the free Wise app, you may convert currencies in real-time while holding up to 50 or more at once.

Reykjavik - Best area for first-timers to stay in Iceland

Iceland's capital and largest city is Reykjavik. This is where most tourists spend at least some of their time when they travel to Iceland, and if this is your first vacation there, this is the greatest place to stay. Reykjavik is a tiny capital city by capital city standards, and most attractions, such as the Harpa Concert Hall, are easily accessible on foot from the downtown area. For this reason, when deciding where to stay in Reykjavik, Iceland, your money will be more important than your location.

Looking for accommodations in Iceland for a week? Reykjavik makes a fantastic base. It is near Iceland's main airport, and Reykjavik is where most day trips depart.

The major thoroughfare in Reykjavik is Laugavegur, where you can find housing, dining, and shopping. You should stay in one of the Reykjavik hotels close to Laugavegur if you want to be in the center of things. If you stay directly on Laugavegur, be aware that you could hear revelers in the small hours. East Town and West Town, which are both

just 20 minutes on foot from the city center, are a little outside of this region.
A PLACE TO STAY IN REYKJAVIK

Reykjavik's Budget Hostels:
Kex Hostel

Reykjavik lodging on a budget:
Hotel Cabin

Mid-Range Accommodations in Reykjavik:
CenterHotel Skjaldbreid

Keflavik - Where to stay near the blue lagoon in Iceland

The most visited tourist destination in Iceland is the renowned Blue Lagoon. You may swim outside in warm waters and try out local spa services at this thermal spring, which is heated by the nearby geothermal plant.

The Blue Lagoon is located near Keflavik, which lies on the Reykjanes Peninsula and is 50 kilometers from Reykjavik. While the majority of tourists to Iceland stay in Reykjavik, Keflavik also has a wide selection of hotels for those who want to be near the Blue Lagoon. The Blue Lagoon is a must-see attraction in Iceland and is about 20 miles from Keflavik. It also has on-site housing.

Where to Stay in Keflavik:

One of the Cheapest Hostels in Keflavik is Guesthouse Keflavik.

Mid-Range Accommodations in Keflavik: Hotel Keflavik and Nupan Deluxe.

Hotels of the highest caliber in Keflavik:
Diamond Suites

Where to stay in the Golden Circle

Just outside of Reykjavik, there is a renowned natural attraction tour known as The Golden Circle. The Thingvellir (Pingvellir) National Park, the Geysir Geothermal Area, the Gullfoss Waterfall, and occasionally the Kerid Crater are places that are often visited.

It makes a fantastic day excursion. Selfoss and Hverageri are wonderful places to rest for the night if you're traveling the Golden Circle but want to remain close by so you can spend more time at each spot. Or they're ideal if you wish to stay longer and visit Iceland's south.

These little villages, which are only 40–50 km from Reykjavik, provide a wide variety of places to stay. Most are often less costly and provide a wide range of eating alternatives than Reykjavik.

AUC 44 Hostel and Hot Springs Hostel are the least expensive places to stay in Selfoss and Hverager, respectively.

Selfoss and Hverageri's mid-range lodging options include Thoristun Apartments, and Hotel ork.

Hotels in Selfoss and Hveragerdi that welcome families: Guesthouse Iceland, Guesthouse Nordheimar, and Guesthouse Frumskogar

Selfoss and Hveragerdi Luxury Budget Hotels: Hotel Ranga, and Ion Adventure Hotel.

Hofn - where to reside near the glacier lagoon in Iceland

Along Iceland's southeast coast is the fishing community of Höfn. It is the closest significant settlement to the Jokulsarlon Glacier Lagoon, the Skaftafell National Park, and Iceland's biggest glacier, Vatnajökull.

Although there may be accommodations available nearer to these locations, Höfn is a nice central position from which to explore this area for a few days or longer. This is also an excellent location for glacier trekking, which is quite popular in Iceland because it cannot be done in nations with warmer climates. Although you may hike on glaciers year-round, the finest seasons are in the summer and fall because of the longer days. Therefore, take Höfn into consideration if you're searching for a place to stay in Iceland in October, September, August, or July.

Best Value Hostels in Höfn:
Hotel Edda Höfn, and Hofn Hostel.

Hotels in Höfn at low prices:
Hofn Guesthouse and Guesthouse Hvammur.

Hofn Inn, Arnanes Country Hotel, Apotek Guesthouse, and Milk Factory are among the mid-priced lodging options.

Hotels in Höfn that welcome families include Hotel Jokull Foss, Dma Studio Apartments and Mikael Hotel.

Egilsstadir - The best place for nature lovers to reside in Iceland

Egilsstadir is the major town where you will find lodging in this area if you are traveling the East Fjords, one of Iceland's more rural regions. In fact, Egilsstadir is located inland along a river, near Hallormsstadur Forest, Iceland's biggest forest, and has access to many significant fjords.

Visitors visiting the East Fjords will only find a limited selection of hotels and hostels in the little hamlet of Egilsstadir, which has fewer than 3,000 people. The fact that Egilsstair has a tiny population and a lot of natural beauty makes it a fantastic site to see animals.

Where to Stay in Egilsstadir:

Tehsi - Café, Bar, Guesthouse & Hostel, One of the Cheapest Hostels in Egilsstadir

Hotels in Egilsstadir that is inexpensive:
Eyjolfsstadir Guesthouse,

Egilsstair's mid-priced lodging options include the Icelandair Hotel, Herad Hotel Edda, and Egilsstadir Guesthouse.

Akureyri – Ring road north in Iceland

One of Iceland's major cities, Akureyri is located in the country's north. This 20,000-person town is conveniently located along Iceland's Ring Road and makes for a nice pit break. Visitors visiting Akureyri will discover museums, cathedrals, botanical gardens, and of course a large number of hotels and restaurants in addition to the natural beauty prevalent across all of Iceland.

Wintertime use of the Ring Road is not advised (at least for visitors!). Therefore, Akureyri and other bigger cities on the Ring Road are the best places to stay in Iceland in September.

Where to Stay in Akureyri: Akureyri Hostel, HI Hafnarstraeti Hostel, Cheapest Hostels in Akureyri

Hotels in Akureyri: Lonsa Guesthouse and Akureyri Guesthouse

Hotels in the middle of the range: Hotel Nordurland by Keahotels Lava Apartments
Torg Hotel Guesthouse

Hotels in Akureyri that welcome families include Hotel Kea by Keahotels and Saeluhus Hotel Akureyri,

Hvolsvollur - Iceland Ring road south

If you want to have time to really stop, participate in activities, and make a few diversions, driving the Iceland Ring Road will take you between 10 and 14 days. You must thus stop at quite a few places along the road. Some of those will be bigger cities with loads of lodging options, while others, like Hvolsvollur, will be a little less traveled.

Although the area is primarily residential, there are a few lodging alternatives including hotels and campgrounds. Although Iceland may appear secluded, you are never too far from another hotel. Being approximately 100 kilometers to the east of Reykjavik, Hvolsvollur is the ideal spot to halt on your journey into or out of the city.

Where to Stay in Hvolsvollur:
Low cost is Borg Apartments.

Hotels in Hvolsvollur's middle range
Midgard Base Camp & Restaurant

Hotels in Hvolsvollur That Accept Families
Guesthouse Vestri-Garsauki

Snaefellsnes Peninsula - Where to stay in Iceland for Adventure

Only 90 km long, the Snaefellsnes Peninsula is home to some of Iceland's most breathtaking landscapes. Visitors to Iceland frequently skip this diversion off the Iceland Ring Road.

However, those who make the effort to travel to the peninsula will be rewarded with beautiful scenery, waterfalls, and a variety of tiny villages from which to choose to spend the night. Although the peninsula lacks major cities, you can still find a few places to stay in places like Helnar, Olavsvik, and Rif.

LODGING OPTIONS ON THE SNAEFELLSNES PENINSULA

The Snaefellsnes Peninsula's cheapest hostels include Hostel B47, Bus Hostel and Hostel Kex Hostel.

Snaefellsnes Peninsula Low-Cost Hotels:
Hotel Cabin

Hotels in the Snæfellsnes Peninsula that welcome family:
CenterHotel Klopp

VIK - Where Should I Stay in Iceland to See the Northern Lights

Even in Reykjavik, Iceland, the Northern Lights may be seen when the conditions are ideal.
Alternatively, if you visit Iceland in the middle of winter, you could be unlucky and never see them at all. In light of this, Vik is the best place to stay if you want to view the Northern Lights in Iceland in November, December, or any of the other gloomier months. It is a small village on Iceland's southern shore that is 180 kilometers from Reykjavik but yet offers a few facilities.

When photographing the Northern Lights, the beaches of Vik's black sand make for an interesting foreground. Just be careful not to visit the black sand beaches at night since it has actually happened that people have been washed away by choppy seas. If you're hesitant, you may join one of the many scheduled tours and Northern Lights tour guides available around Iceland.

Where to Stay in Vik:

Low cost: The Barn

Hotel Edda Vik and Guesthouse are, a mid-range lodging option in Vik

Hotels in Vik that welcome families:
Hótel Kria

Husavik - Stay here for Christmas

Where to Stay in Husavik, Iceland, During the Holidays
You should spend Christmas in a Nordic nation at least once to get a true sense of what a snowy Christmas should be like. And while every town in Iceland may provide you with a beautiful winter paradise, Husavik is the best place to stay if you're seeking accommodations in Iceland in December.

On Iceland's north coast, there is a sizable fishing community that the residents really deck up for the holidays. If you wish to go to a service to sing carols, there is a beautiful wooden church that is the town's most recognizable structure. Alternative: Hear some Icelandic-sung holiday music! Additionally, you may eat holiday pastries at cafés and bakeries.

LOCATIONS IN HUSAVIK

Husavik's Budget Backpacker Hostels (Hotel Husavik Green)

Hotels on a budget in Husavik
(Skógar Sunset Guesthouse and Höfi Guesthouse)

Hotels in Husavik's Average price
(Arból Guesthouse, Fosshótel and Laugarholt
Apartment)

Hotels in Husavik that welcome families
(Post-Plaza Guesthouse, Askja Apartment and
Husavik Cape Hotel, and Sólheimar Apartment)

Cheap Luxury Hotels
(Apartments in Husavik Skjalfandi)

Laugarvatn - Where to stay in Iceland for couples

A little town called Laugarvatn lies near Iceland's Golden Circle Route. There isn't much there, just a few places to stay and a grocery store, but it's ideal for couples looking for peace and privacy on a romantic couples' getaway.

A lovely swimming pool with a geothermal spa on the side of a lake is one of Laugarvatn's attractions. There are never any crowds because very few visitors are aware that it exists, and if you're lucky, you could even have the place to yourself!

LODGING OPTIONS IN LAUGARVATN

Most affordable backpacker hostels in Laugarvatn (Hotel Laugarvatn)

Laugarvatn Low-Cost Hotels
(Háholt, Bjork Guesthouse and Farmhotel Efstidalur)

Hotels in Laugarvatn's average price
(Galleri Laugarvatn)

Family-friendly lodging options in Laugarvatn

(Gistiheimili Björk, and Middalskot Cottages)

Where to Stay Outside of the Reykjavik/Keflavik International Airport

Reykjavik Airport is not Iceland's primary international airport, despite what many tourists believe. There is an airport in Reykjavik, however, it does not serve international flights. Keflavik International Airport, located about 50 kilometers west of Reykjavik, is the true international airport for Iceland.

No matter where you stay in Iceland, you may reserve a lot of airport transfers straight via your hotel. However, you might want to stay a little closer if you have an especially early departure out of Iceland or a late flight into Iceland. Reykjanesbaer is ideal since Keflavik Airport is located just next door. Even activities to do like visiting museums, eateries, and bakeries are available here.

Where to Stay in Reykjanesbaer: Start Hostel, the Most Affordable Backpacking Hostel

Reykjanesbaer Low-Cost Hotels Kef Guesthouse and Hotel Grásteinn

Mid-range lodging options in Reykjanesbaer include Nupan Deluxe and Ace Guesthouse.

Reykjanesbaer, Iceland - The Viking World Museum exhibits an ancient Icelandic hunt. Viking World has a zoo, a playground, and an outdoor school in addition to its five exhibitions.

Best Dishes To Try Out While on your Vacation

Pure beauty and breathtaking nature are your constant companions everywhere you go in Iceland. It is not surprising that this beautiful nation has so much to offer, including a feast for the senses as well as a feast for the eyes. Here are the top 10 regional cuisines from Iceland that you should try!

TASTING FOOD IN ICELAND WILL BE THE HIGHLIGHT OF YOUR TRIP

Your eyes will be opened to a vast array of genuine flavors and meals as you try new delicacies and sensations you have never experienced before. You might perhaps be in for some of the most delectable experiences here in Iceland! The world's healthiest cuisine is Icelandic. The highest quality food you've ever had may be made with ingredients like air and water that are both crystal pure, sheep and cows that are allowed to graze freely, wild fish, and chemical-free vegetation.

A crucial contribution is that a nation's cuisine reflects not just its tastes but also its culture and history. Particularly in the case of Iceland! Discovering the local cuisine is the most interesting method to learn about Icelandic history since it engages all of your senses.

The greatest thing is that you can take the Golden Circle Local Food Trip, a fantastic one-day tour, to sample the majority of these meals as well as see Iceland's most well-known natural attractions. Let us demonstrate the most intriguing and distinctive Icelandic cuisine that you absolutely must sample when visiting the country.

THE ICELANDIC YOGURT (SKYR)

A very well-known Icelandic product is called skyr. It has been a staple of Icelandic cooking for more than a millennium. Skyr is a cultured dairy product that has a yogurt-like texture. Although it has a milder flavor than Greek yogurt, they are extremely comparable.

Skyr is often consumed by Icelanders with milk and fruit or berries, but it is also frequently used in smoothies, ice cream, and the lighter "skyrkaka," a favorite substitute for cheesecake. Even though Skyr is sometimes mistaken for yogurt, it is actually a soft cheese.

Skyr has recently grown in favor in other nations, where it is more common at grocery shops in nations like the United States and England.

LAMB SLOW-ROASTED

One of the cleanest breeds of sheep in the world is Icelandic. Since the first immigrants brought them to Iceland in the ninth century, they have been grazing on the country's highlands.

In Iceland, growth hormones and grain are not given to lambs. From spring through autumn, they are able to travel outdoors, thus their diet is entirely natural and consists of grass, sedge, moss campion, and berries. One of Iceland's best and most often used culinary components is Icelandic sheep meat, which is widely regarded as gourmet meat. On menus for celebratory dinners or on Christmas Day, lamb is frequently an ingredient.

Icelanders typically roast a leg of lamb for several hours at a low temperature in the oven with fresh herbs, notably blóberg (Arctic thyme). Cooking it in a geothermally heated pit in the earth for many hours was the authentic Icelandic method!

Today, preparing a beautiful leg of lamb couldn't be easier. Simply season a 2.2 to 2.5-kilogram leg of lamb with your preferred fresh herbs and seasoning (marjoram, oregano, basil, sage, parsley, garlic, salt, and pepper), and set it in an oven that has been preheated to 200° C. Depending on how well done you want it, cook it for a further 60 to 75 minutes after lowering the temperature to 180° C after 30 to 40 minutes.

As soon as the heat is reduced, the higher temperature sears the skin. You should check on the meat occasionally and cover it with foil or a lid if the skin is getting too crisp or the herbs are burning. Keep an eye on everything because every oven is different!

Simply purchase lamb filets, which you can cook in 30 to 40 minutes at 200° C. If you'd like, you can even purchase lamb filets that have already been marinated.

SHARK FERMENTED (HAKARL)

Icelandic cuisine traditionally includes hákarl. Shark meat has undergone a specific fermentation procedure to cure it, after which it has been hung outside to dry for four to five months. It tastes strongly like fish and has an overpowering ammonia smell.

Hákarl is frequently served on cocktail sticks cut into cubes. When eating their first bite, beginners are encouraged to pinch their nostrils because the fragrance is actually much greater than the taste! Do like the Icelanders do and take a few nice sips of brennivin, a sort of aquavit sometimes referred to as Icelandic schnapps, after your first meal.

The shark that has been fermented is not a dish that locals frequently consume these days. Most individuals who give it a try consider it to be really disgusting. Back when they didn't have refrigeration or many other food alternatives, Icelanders used to consume hákarl. Even though this dish may not be the most delicious, it is a typical local cuisine that is distinctive of Iceland and something you must taste when you visit.

ICELANDIC LAMB SOUP (KJÖTSÚPA)

A specialty of Iceland is lamb soup. It has been consumed in Iceland for millennia and is growing in popularity among tourists.

This hearty, flavorful soup is the ideal comfort dish for a long, gloomy winter day. Traditional Icelandic meat soup is made with lamb shank or shoulder, potatoes, rutabagas (swede), and carrots, though every family has their own recipe for it. Leeks, onions, dried herbs, salt, and pepper are additional possible ingredients.

ICELAND FISH

There are 340 species of saltwater fish known to exist in Icelandic waters, making it a fisherman's paradise. The most popular saltwater species include:

Atlantic catfish and wolffish
Capelin
Icelandic shark
Haddock
Lumpsucker
Mackerel
Pollock

The rivers and lakes are home to three different species of salmon:

Atlantic salmon Arctic char
Black trout
When visiting Iceland, you should make an effort to consume as much Icelandic seafood as you can. It is not only incredibly beneficial to your health but also delicious! Simply seek the "fish of the day" option on the menu at many restaurants to get fish that was caught that day. There is no fresher than that!

ICELAND HOT DOG

You may already be familiar with the renowned Icelandic Hot Dog. Over time, this apparently commonplace foodstuff has become famous all over the world; Bill Clinton once infamously referred to them as "the tastiest hot dogs in the world."

The Baejarins Beztu Pylsur is the most well-known and often visited "restaurant" in Iceland. People frequently wait in a big queue to enjoy this treat. Don't pass up the chance to eat a hot dog when you are in Iceland since, despite their notoriety, they are really inexpensive!

DARK RYE (Rúgbrauð)

Icelanders have been enjoying Rúgbrauð, a traditional rye bread, for a long time. It is often steamed in unique wooden barrels that have been buried in the ground next to a hot spring or cooked in a pot.

This bread has no crust and is thick, dark brown, and sweet in flavor. Butter, smoked salmon mutton pâté, hangikjöt (smoked lamb), pickled herring, or cheese go well with it. This bread is frequently consumed by Icelanders as a side dish to the traditional fish meal. This bread is available in the majority of Icelandic supermarkets.

DRIED FISH (HARDFISKUR)

Most inhabitants in Iceland like hardfiskur, which literally translates to "hard fish." Although many visitors might find it disgusting, it is Iceland's preferred food. Locals enjoy it while watching movies and eat it with salted butter. It is seen as a more nutritious option than chips or popcorn.

For ages, hardfiskur has been a staple of Icelandic cuisine. Haddock or wolffish may also be used, however, cod is the most popular ingredient. It is aged like cheese by being dried in the chilly North Atlantic air until it is cured by bacteria.

Many people consume fish plain, full of protein, as a nutritious snack. However, some prefer to slather it with copious amounts of butter. You ought to give it a go.

BAKERY

Make sure to enjoy a brief stop at a local bakery if you visit Iceland. You should taste some of the amazing bakery dishes in Iceland. The soft cinnamon bun known as the Icelandic Snúður typically has icing on top.

In Iceland, Kleina is arguably the most well-known pastry from Scandinavia. When dining out in Iceland, bakeries are a cost-effective alternative, and their goods are undoubtedly excellent!

ICELAND ICE-CREAM

Ice cream is a national obsession in Iceland. Frost, whether it is in the winter or the summer, may even enhance the experience. Most cafés and petrol stations sell it, and there are also some wonderful specialty ice cream stores scattered over the nation.

Some ice cream shops stay open till one in the morning so that customers may enjoy their treats then. There is a huge variety of ice creams available with several different toppings and sauces. Include an Icelandic ice cream on your bucket list, please!

CHAPTER 3

Best Time To Travel To Get The Most Refreshing Experience

The summer months of June through August are the ideal time to visit Iceland. During this time, the nation has longer daylight hours (the "midnight sun") and milder temperatures. Iceland is also beautiful in the winter if you want to see the Northern Lights, but you should be ready for shorter days and colder weather.

Iceland is undoubtedly a year-round destination, but it's important to note that the landscapes drastically change from summer to winter. The warmer spring and summer months are perhaps the best if you want to be active in the lush countryside and have plenty of daylight to observe wildlife and waterfalls. Would you rather relax in geothermal baths while having the opportunity to view the Northern Lights in all their splendor? The optimum time for you would probably be during the cooler months with their longer evenings. Before deciding whether to fly to Iceland, we've broken down some of the key variables.

When to travel to Iceland to view the Golden Circle

The Golden Circle is a popular tourist route that connects some of the most renowned natural attractions in the nation, including Thingvellir National Park, the Geysir Geothermal Area, and Gullfoss Waterfall. It is easily accessible from Reykjavik in both winter and summer. All of these sights are open all year, but what you see can be very different. Freshwater streams meander through lush green meadows in Thingvellir throughout the summer, but during the winter the park is covered in snow, the streams freeze over, and even the large Thingvallavatn Lake partially freezes over. At the Geysir, clear summer days are ideal for viewing eruptions, but winter is when you'll really feel the intense heat that's churning below you. At Gullfoss, the river is bordered by lush rocky meadows in the summer, and the falls erupt out of nowhere before disappearing from view. During the winter, the falls create frozen chunks along the boundaries of the fields, which are blanketed in white.

When should one travel to Iceland to view the Northern Lights

Each year, the Aurora Borealis, also known as the Northern Lights, appears from late September to late march. Iceland has longer, darker evenings throughout the winter; however, cloudier skies may accompany this change, which may reduce your view. Like with any natural occurrence, there are no assurances or set times, but if you go to the right spot at the right time, you might see one of the most incredible nightlights of your life!

When to go to see Iceland at its greenest

If lush scenery and warm weather appeal to you, spring and summer are the greatest and most perfect periods to visit Iceland. The days are warmer in the early spring, while the summer has extended daytime hours with few evenings. The hottest months, July and August, are also the busiest for travelers. However, keep in mind that the length of the day is quite lengthy during the summer. Even in the hottest part of the day, when the sun sets for almost three hours, there is still some light in the sky.

When should you go to Iceland to avoid crowds

If you don't like long lines, crowds, and higher-than-normal costs, the shoulder seasons, or off-seasons, in Iceland are around Autumn (September to November) and the middle of Spring (April to May). September is often a slower month for tourism because of the changing weather and perhaps more difficult access to the countryside. Off-peak travelers may still enjoy a lot of things, such as the splendor of the fall foliage and, of course, the beginning of the Aurora.

What To Pack For Iceland Trip

The weather in Iceland is as diverse as its breathtaking scenery. Whether you're planning a city getaway or a self-drive trip through isolated rural locations, use the fast advice below to pack shrewdly and keep warm and dry.

ESSENTIALS FOR EVERY SEASON
No matter what time of year you're going, the following is an example packing list of things to bring:

A lightweight wool sweater with a fleece jacket.

Windproof/rainproof outerwear.

Rain gear.

Dependable walking shoes with strong tread and traction.

Gloves.

Scarves.

Hat (beanie/toque).

Swimsuit.

For use during activities or travel in the highlands, thermal underwear.

Footwear for hiking that is waterproof (especially for activities or travel in the highlands)

Warm socks (especially for activities and travel in the highlands and winter)

Swift-drying towel (for visiting pools and hot springs - towels are available for rent at swimming facilities)

Packing advice for summer

Eye shades may be useful since some guests find it difficult to fall asleep in the glare of the midnight sun. Additionally, sunscreen and sunglasses are advised. Iceland has few insects, however, little midges do well in the summer, particularly around lakes and streams.

Those visiting the Lake Myvatn region in the summer may also want to pack bug repellent, fly masks, or fly nets (especially useful for horse riding).

Winter packing guidelines

Although it does not frequently get below freezing in Iceland during the winter, it is nevertheless advisable to wear an insulated jacket because of the chilly northerly winds. For typical temperatures, see our Weather guide.

You might also want to bring ice cleats, ice grips, or anti-slip soles for your shoes because walkways can become icy and treacherous. In Iceland, you can also buy them from a variety of retailers, including ones that sell outdoor apparel.

Visiting the town

Reykjavik is a cosmopolitan metropolis like any other European capital, even if clothing restrictions are rarely enforced. If you intend to venture out in Reykjavik, whether to have a bite to eat or to experience the city's renowned nightlife, we advise that you bring decent clothing and a pair of shoes to wear.

Not to worry. Downtown Reykjavik is home to a number of clothing boutiques and secondhand stores. One of them is flying Tiger, a low-cost department store offering a wide selection of accessories at low prices, including batteries, gloves, earplugs, and sunglasses.

H&M has men's, women's, and children's items at Austurbakki 2 in downtown Reykjavik, including affordable swimwear, socks, and undergarments. Numerous worldwide high-street brands are also present in the Kringlan shopping area, which is only a few kilometers from the city center.

Remain warm and dry.

Icelandic clothing shop. A large variety of apparel is available at 66° North for any weather Iceland may bring. Visit 66North.com if you want to dress like an Icelander.

After crossing the North Atlantic, if you start to feel chilly or damp, we suggest stopping by one of their stores on Bankastraeti in Reykjavik, or in the Kringlan or Smáralind malls.

Keep your receipts for whatever you bought in Iceland so you can get your money back when you leave!

In aid of a lighter load

For your everyday necessities (such as a camera, wallet, prescriptions, additional layers of clothes, a bottle of water, etc.), we advise taking a rucksack or small bag as you might not have easy access to your suitcase during the day as you move between hotels. Additionally, it is useful for picnics and trekking expeditions.

Horse riders

For horseback riding trips in Iceland, full equipment is given, including a loan of boots, helmets, and overalls. It is completely banned to import any second hand horse riding equipment or apparel

from other countries to Iceland in order to
safeguard Icelandic horses from dangerous
infections.

CHAPTER 4

5 Days' Vacation In Iceland

The Golden Circle, the South Coast, and Reykjavik are all popular choices for first-time travelers with only 5 days in Iceland.

These things taken together can create a fantastic five-day Iceland itinerary.

First Day: Reykjavik

In order to pass the time before you can check into your lodgings if you are coming early, you might wish to schedule a stop at the Blue Lagoon on your trip to Reykjavik. I personally think the Blue Lagoon is very commercial, but I'm aware that for many, visiting Iceland wouldn't be complete without seeing the Blue Lagoon. The crowds won't be too awful if you arrive really early in the morning.

You might also try the more recent Sky Lagoon, which is closer to the city and gives stunning views of the water as an option. You may also reserve a ticket that includes transfers if you don't have a car.

Get some lunch after settling into your lodgings, then stroll down the shoreline to see the Sun Voyager sculpture before heading over to the breathtaking Harpa Concert Hall. Make sure to explore the space inside to admire the stunning architecture and light bouncing off the glass.

Take a short stroll to the Old Harbor after visiting the Harpa to take a Puffin Expedited boat excursion or an express whale viewing cruise. The puffin trip lasts only an hour, allowing you plenty of time to explore and see these endearing tiny birds. You should stop at Icelandic Fish & Chips for dinner because you will have worked up an appetite.

Visit the Perlan is a fantastic alternative if it's too chilly to go out on the sea. The ice cave and planetarium display in this glass dome structure will give you the impression that you are viewing the Northern Lights. If you just have a short amount of time in Iceland but yet want to experience some of its enchantment, this is a fantastic alternative.

A visit to the Whales of Iceland exhibit downtown is another option, especially for those who miss out on a whale-watching cruise. The interactive exhibitions and 23 life-size whale reproductions are especially appealing to children.

Spend some time exploring and shopping on Laugavegur, the major shopping street, following the afternoon activities, and then take the elevator to the top of the Hallgrimskirkja cathedral for stunning city views.

Second Day: Golden Circle

Take advantage of Sandholt Bakery's delicious breakfast to start off your second day. Icelandic Street Food is a fantastic substitute if the queue is too lengthy there.

In order to avoid having to change hotels every night, I advise spending the second day seeing the Golden Circle and maintaining Reykjavik as your home base. I suggest choosing Hidden Iceland if you want to go on a small group trip.

Plan to complete the Golden Circle counterclockwise, beginning at the 6,500-year-old Kerid Crater for a brief stroll around the caldera if you want to avoid the large tour buses at each destination. You can next decide to schedule a trip at the Secret Lagoon for a more rural and natural hot spring setting.

Another well-liked stop along the Golden Circle road is Fridheimar, a restaurant and tomato farm where the greenhouses where Iceland's fresh salads are grown are heated by geothermal energy. Ensure that you reserve a table for lunch in advance.

The magnificent Gullfoss waterfall will be your next visit. Give yourself enough time to explore the several vantage points and observe the twin rainbows that frequently appear over the waterfall. Although many consider this to be Iceland's most stunning waterfall, you will see my personal favorite tomorrow.

Just 10 minutes down the road from Gullfoss, you can find the Geysir Visitor Center. Parking here will let you see the dependable Strokkur geyser erupt while you cross the street. I like that you can approach near even if it isn't as towering and stunning as Old Faithful in Yellowstone. A huge blue bubble develops just before it bursts into a jet of steam and water that shoots skyward. Although this visit normally shouldn't take too long, you can take your time wandering around the hot pots.

Include a trip to the Laugarvatn Fontana spa if you have time in your schedule for a swim in their pools and a tour of their thermal bakery.

You may stop at Efstidalur II, a farm guesthouse and restaurant with fantastic homemade ice cream, or you can have a late lunch there. Efstidalur II is located at Blaskogabyggd 801.

Your day should come to an end in Thingvellir National Park, the first Parliament of Iceland. Additionally, it serves as a location for Game of Thrones filming and offers a view of the chasm that separates the two continents. Although the views aren't particularly impressive, this is an excellent location if you want to go trekking. By this time of day, you are usually tired of getting in and out of the car and would probably prefer a brief stop.

For supper, you may either head back to Reykjavik or stop in Lindin at Lindarbraut in Laugarvatn. Although not the most kid-friendly restaurant, Lindin specializes in fish (such as whale and puffin) and game (such as reindeer burgers), and it was fine for our foodie family.

Third Day: South Coast

On your third day, you should plan to check out of your hotel early and get a hotel room for the next night or two in the Vik region, ideally close to the Glacier Lagoon. The South Coast's most stunning locations will be the focus of this long and hectic day. Before you go, make sure to load up on food.

To make the most of your day, leave Reykjavik early and take Rt 1 (the Ring Road) east for about an hour and a half before turning into Rt 249 to reach the Seljalandsfoss waterfall. As you approach the waterfall, you will be able to see it and don't be shocked if you also notice a lot of tour buses. However, bear in mind that even when Iceland is packed, it is nothing like the throngs you would find somewhere like Niagara Falls. Ideally, you can slip in there between the bus tours and experience the falls without the crowds.

You can go behind the waterfall at Seljalandsfoss, which is one of the best things I've ever done and one of the attractions there. I wouldn't recommend doing this in the winter as the area surrounding the waterfall is pure ice and you will need crampons or microspikes if you want to get close. Just be sure to wear good non-slip, waterproof shoes as well as a raincoat and rain pants because even getting close to the falls will result in you getting wet from the mist.

The Gljufrabui waterfall may be reached by continuing on the trail a few hundred meters along the cliff face after passing behind the falls. To access this secret waterfall, you must squeeze through a narrow gap in the rock and cross a little creek. This undiscovered gem is missed by so many tourists on bus tours, yet it was a highlight of our vacation! Unless you don't mind having chilly, wet feet for the rest of the day, you will need some nice waterproof hiking shoes to enter, though.

If you're hungry, Seljalandsfoss frequently has a food truck or a fish and chip stand set up.

After you've gotten your fill of Seljalandsfoss, travel another 30 minutes north on Rt 1 to reach Skogafoss in Skogar. You may go to the base of the falls and then take a stairway up to get a better view of them. This waterfall, in my opinion, is the most stunning one in the five days we spend in Iceland. Just be sure to allow yourself enough time to take in the falls! You would anticipate that these will just be quick photo opportunities, but the waterfalls are so stunning that you'll want to take some time to simply take it all in.

After finishing, go down Rt. 1 to Rt. 218 for 35 minutes to reach Dyrhólaey, a sea arch made of stone where puffins breed. To get to Dyrhólaey, you'll have to go up a treacherous, winding dirt road. Just be aware that this region is closed from late May to early June for puffin nesting. We were lucky since it was open when we went, and by slightly leaning over the cliff, we were able to get up and personal with these adorable young puffins. Just be extremely careful because the cliff edge lacks guardrails and the wind may be fairly powerful. On the promontory, there is a charming lighthouse as well.

Return to Rt. 1 and take it to Rt. 215 to reach Reynisfjara (30 minutes away), which has a black sand beach as well as spectacular basalt columns, caverns, and sea stacks. A recent rockfall may have caused a section of the beach to shut. In any event, keep away from the water's edge as there are frequently hazardous rogue waves here. You shouldn't skip seeing this famous location in Iceland.

There is a tiny café nearby that serves a mouthwatering version of the traditional Icelandic meal beef soup.

If you haven't eaten yet, enjoy lunch in Vik before visiting the well-known Reynisdrangur rock formations on the black sand beach. To feel the "fire" component of the Land of Ice and Fire, I would also suggest seeing the brand-new Icelandic Lava Show.

To limit traveling around, you can decide to spend two or three nights in this approximate location on the south coast. Several possibilities are:

Hotel Ranga Midgard Base Camp Hotel Vik I Myrdal Volcano Hotel

You may stop for supper at Systrakaffi at Klaustur Vergi 13, 880 Kirkjubaejarklaustri if you're going to the Glacier Lagoon this day. In addition to basic cuisine like pizza and hamburgers, this charming cafe has fancier specialties like an exceptionally well-prepared arctic char. This is a wonderful place to search for an Airbnb if you can't locate accommodations close to the glacier or nearer Vik.

Drive over the lava fields to the Jökulsárlón Lagoon if you're staying close to the glacial lagoon.

Fourth Day: Glacier hiking and icebergs

Start your journey from the south coast by driving east to the Jökulsárlón Lagoon. Although you may view icebergs from the shore, I advise taking a boat excursion to get a closer look. If you don't have little children, a zodiac boat trip will allow you to go close to all kinds of icebergs and the glacier face.

Diamond Beach may be reached by crossing the bridge that connects the lagoon to the ocean. Large shards of ice that wash up on the coast and shine like diamonds on the black sand beach gave it its name.

You may visit during the winter and enjoy an ice cave tour instead. However, unless you have a lot of experience driving in the winter, I wouldn't advise coming out here by yourself.

After finishing at the Lagoon, you may continue on your way back to Reykjavik or Keflavik by stopping once more along the South Coast.

I'd suggest going on a glacier trek in the late afternoon. In Skaftafell National Park, you may trek on a glacier close to the glacier lagoon. We went on a three-hour glacier trek with Arcanum Tours throughout our excursion.

Fifth Day: South Coast / Reykjanes Peninsula

You still have one more day of adventure left if you stay in Iceland for five full days before returning home. On the other hand, if your flight leaves late on the fifth day, you ought to start traveling in the direction of Keflavik and do a self-guided tour of the Reykjanes Peninsula before going to the airport.

If you have children, take them to the Viking World Museum, which is close to the airport in Keflavik, where they can witness an exact copy of a Viking ship that traveled from Iceland to Canada and the United States. You can study Norse mythology and Viking history. A small playground and petting zoo are located outside.

Take an extra day to enjoy some more activities along the south coast, though, if your flight doesn't leave until your sixth day. A few examples are as follows:

Horseback riding on the black sand beach in Vik
Super Jeep tours in the Thorsmork Valley ATV rides on the black sand beach
I hope you leave Iceland just as amazed, fatigued, and in love with this magnificent place as we did.

Visiting Iceland On a Budget

We're going to give our best financial advice for visiting Iceland in this chapter to help you plan a budget-friendly trip. To help you travel to Iceland on a budget, we'll start by providing you with an idea of what goods cost there and how to create a budget for your trip. Then, we'll give 21 different budget recommendations. We discuss strategies to cut costs in Iceland on travel, lodging, auto rentals, eating out, camping, drinking, shopping, gas, and sightseeing.

This chapter will assist you in making the most of your money and your vacation to Iceland, whether you are traveling on a $1,000 or a $10,000 budget.

What Are Prices Like in Iceland?

Iceland utilizes the Icelandic krona (ISK), thus before you know the exchange range, and make sure to verify the krona's current rates against your local currency. Additionally, you should be aware of current prices for goods and services.

We suggest visiting the website Numbeo (Search Google "numbeo Iceland") to get a good general sense of what goods are currently costing in Iceland. Here, you may look at the cost of essential items like bananas, a pair of Levi jeans, fuel, meals at a restaurant, and wine by nation or by city.

Food products

The cost of groceries is now among the highest in the world in Iceland. Here are some typical costs: 1 kilogram of fresh white bread (357 ISK; $2.77), a bottle of mid-range red wine (2400 ISK; $18.62), 1 kg of white rice (330 ISK; $2.56), and 1 kg of boneless chicken breasts (2050 ISK; $15.90) are also included in the price.

Restaurants

Hot dogs cost 450 ISK (USD $3.49) at a hot dog stand, 12-inch Subway subs cost 1089 ISK (USD $8.45), hamburgers cost 1,750 ISK (USD $13.57) at a gas station, and a two-course meal (without beverages) for two people costs 12,000 ISK (USD $93) at a mid-range restaurant.

Travel & Recreation

Prices vary widely depending on the sort of trip, its duration, and its features, but to give you an idea, the following are some typical costs (per person): A 1-hour puffin viewing boat cruise from Reykjavik costs 6100 ISK (USD $48), a full-day Golden Circle sightseeing bus tour costs 8,700 ISK (USD $68), a 2-hour snorkeling trip costs 19,300 ISK (USD $150), and an ice cave tour costs 20,000 ISK (USD $157). For multi-day trips, the rates are 71,000 ISK (USD $556) for a three-day, two-night trip; 206,000 ISK (USD $1,600); or 240,000 (USD $1870) for an eight-night, seven-night trip.

Hotels

Prices vary greatly depending on location and season, with summer costs sometimes doubling those in the winter. Reykjavik is much more expensive than the countryside. However, we do offer some ballpark typical pricing. A bed in a shared dorm costs 3,800 ISK (USD $30) at a budget hostel, 6,500 ISK (USD $50) in a fancier hostel, etc. 75 dollars for a private guesthouse room at 9,600 ISK, Budget hotels and guesthouses cost 12,800 ISK (USD $100), mid-range hotels cost 20,000 ISK (USD $157), and luxury hotels cost above 30,000 ISK (USD $230+) for a room.

Campgrounds

A minor overnight fee, which is presently set at 333 ISK (USD $2.78) for each tent or campervan, is added to the cost of a campsite, which ranges from 1,000 to 2,600 ISK (USD $8 to $20) per person/night. For usage of supplementary services like laundry, rubbish disposal, and showers, there are sometimes minimal additional expenses.

Entry Fees at Museums

Entry fees to museums and other attractions often run between 800 ISK (USD $6.20) and 2500 ISK (USD $19.39). Reykjavik has the most costly museums, although prices are lower outside of popular tourist destinations.

Rental Vehicles

Although rates for renting a car might vary, the following basic figures will help you plan your budget: A modest campervan with a roof tent costs 15,700 ISK (USD $120/day), a small 4X4 Jeep costs 10,300 ISK (USD $80/day), and luxury automobiles and Jeeps cost 16,700+ (USD $130+/day).

All rentals typically come with obligatory insurance (commonly referred to as basic CDW), however, you may often pay an additional 2,000 to 2,500 ISK ($17 to $21)/day to upgrade to include physical damage/gravel coverage. Here you can compare the costs of renting automobiles and RVs in Iceland.

Petroleum

A liter of fuel is projected to cost 317 ISK (USD $2.88). Keep in mind that 1 liter only equates to around 1/4 of a gallon. Fuel costs 1,268 ISK (US $11.52) per gallon.

Transportation in the public

In Reykjavik, a one-way standard adult bus ticket costs 480 ISK (USD $3.72), however, if you ride the bus frequently, a bus pass can help you save money. The public city buses in Akureyri are free to ride. Price ranges for long-distance bus tickets vary depending on location and season, but one from Reykjavik to Akureyri is likely to go between 8,000 ISK and 11,000 ISK (USD $62 to $85).

Budget-Friendly Iceland financial advice on how to save costs

Iceland is so expensive; why?
Icelandic prices are high for a number of reasons. Although Iceland has one of the highest living costs in the world, it doesn't simply affect tourists.

The difficulty and expense of importing products into Iceland, an island in the North Atlantic, contributes to the country's high pricing. The fact that Iceland is a tiny nation with a limited workforce and high living expenses is another factor driving up labor prices. Additionally, the nation must rely on employing foreign workers, particularly in the fishing and tourist industries.

Taxes and import fees are additional considerations for some products. For instance, Iceland has unusually high taxes on both alcohol and fuel.

However, the nation's currency is also a significant consideration. The Icelandic krona and economy were both in pretty good shape when we last visited (some were saying it was too strong). Naturally, this results in extremely expensive costs for everything. However, the krona collapses and prices fall when the nation has a recession or financial crisis (like in 2008).

Therefore, as a traveler, the costs you incur will be significantly influenced by Iceland's economic performance. It would be wise to check this out before your trip because your budget might be drastically incorrect if you use price predictions from six months ago.

Budget-Friendly Iceland financial advice on how to save costs
One of the cheapest locations to get a sandwich is Subway.
Advice on Creating Your Own Budget for Iceland
Set a reasonable travel budget using the information you have gathered.

Ideally, a budget should:

1.) Be thorough - Include all of your key trip expenses, such as your flights, housing, meals, transportation (buses, rental cars, ferries, etc.), excursions and activities, entrance fees to attractions, and extras (e.g., shopping, souvenirs, camping gear rental).

2. Keep in mind that Iceland's costs are often high.

3.) Take a seat comfortably within your means. Make sure to include a little extra for unforeseen costs.

4.) Avoid being overly rigid. Don't schedule a trip that is so financially constrained that you have second thoughts about whether you'll be able to thoroughly enjoy it.

What if I'm unable to afford a trip to Iceland?

Consider taking a shorter vacation (e.g., 3 days instead of 5 days) or delaying your trip until you have saved up some money if you discover after conducting some pricing research and reviewing our budgeting advice that you have serious worries about the expenditures. Next year, Iceland will still be present.

You don't want the stress of thinking about money while traveling, nor do you want to feel so constrained that the experience is devoid of enjoyment. For instance, would you still appreciate Iceland if you were limited to eating cooked rice every night and had no access to any paid activities?

Establish the amount of money you must save, then calculate how long it will take you to accumulate that amount for your trip. The ideal approach is to make little weekly (or monthly) savings increments until you attain your savings target.

1. Iceland Off-Season Travel

The summer season is the busiest and most costly time to visit Iceland. Mid-June until the end of August roughly corresponds to the Icelandic peak season. During this time, prices for hotels, attractions, car rentals, and other services are frequently higher. We visited in both the summer and the winter, and the rise in hotel rates was very evident. Expect increasing prices as demand increases.

Therefore, if your vacation plans are flexible, think about going somewhere else in the summer, especially in July and August. By avoiding the most expensive and busiest times in Iceland, you'll also save money. If you still want to go during this time, think about going in late May, early June, or September, which is just outside the busiest time.

There is a reason why most visitors want to go in the summer, despite the greater costs. This is partially due to the fact that this is when most people can take their vacations, but it is also the time of year when Iceland has its finest weather conditions and the majority of its tourist-oriented establishments, activities, and services are available. Summer is the finest season to observe wildlife in Iceland, and it is also the safest period for travel, hiking, and camping. So while making a decision, consider both the advantages and disadvantages.

2. Purchase a Budget Flight

In order to save money for your vacation, try to get low-cost airline tickets. You can certainly obtain cheap plane tickets if you reside in North America (especially the Midwestern or Eastern United

States), Western Europe, or Northern Europe. You should be able to locate good flights if you are persistent and have open dates.

Icelandair, the primary airline serving Iceland, and Play are the principal suppliers of low-cost flights to Iceland (budget-focused airline). Prior to March 2019, WOW Air served as the low-cost airline in Iceland.

For instance, round-trip airfare to Reykjavik in the UK starts at USD $180, while Americans from a small number of places may occasionally get deals on round-trip airfare from the east coast to Reykjavk starting at USD $200!

Just be careful to double-check the airline's baggage policies as most low-cost carriers have stringent weight and luggage restrictions. If necessary, you'll need to factor extra baggage costs into the price of your ticket. An Icelandair Economy Light ticket, for instance, does not support any checked bags.

Because they did not pre-pay, a lot of travelers wind up having to pay expensive additional luggage fees at the airport. If you need to bring more luggage, you may save money by purchasing the extra baggage allowance when you buy your ticket rather than at the airport.

If you want to take advantage of low tickets but don't reside in a nation or close to a city where Icelandair or Play operates, you can consider booking a flight that links to one of those places. We enjoy using Priceline, Kiwi, and Southwest to book flights (for flights within the USA only).

On their trip from North America to Europe or the other way around, many travelers stop in Iceland. On the majority of transatlantic flights operated by Icelandair, stopovers are free of charge, and you can remain in Iceland for one to seven days. If you merely want to see the attractions of Iceland and it is not your major vacation destination, a stopover is a fantastic option to experience the country. For additional inspiration, see our guide to stopping in Iceland.

NOTICE: Keflavik Foreign Airport, located roughly 30 miles southwest of Reykjavik, is now the landing point for all international flights. Reykjavik has an airport, however, it is primarily utilized for domestic flights (and a few from Greenland & the Faroe Islands).

3. Examine lodging choices

By contrasting several housing possibilities and browsing various websites, you may save money.

Hostels, guesthouses, flats, and hotels are just a few of the accommodation possibilities in Iceland. Reykjavik offers the most hotel alternatives, with establishments ranging from cheap to luxurious. Fewer options are available in less populous parts of the nation. In all regions of the nation, guesthouses, bed-and-breakfasts, and small hotels are the most prevalent lodging options.

When making your own hotel reservations, be careful to shop about and take other possibilities into account.

To start, check out these locations to get a sense of prices:

Booking.com

One of the biggest and most popular online travel agencies, it provides a wide range of lodging choices, including hotels, guesthouses, vacation rentals, flats, and hostels. We often reserve our hotel using this service from anywhere in the world.

HostelWorld

Our suggested website for finding and reserving hostels worldwide. In Iceland, hostels are frequently the least expensive choice (except for campsites).

Vrbo

A well liked website where you may locate houses for rent, flats, and vacation properties. Be aware that Iceland, like many other countries, has a big number of illegal holiday rental homes, and that over the past few years, the number of these properties has grown significantly, pushing up locals' rent costs. As a result, some Icelanders frequently dislike these services!

4. Reserve lodging in advance

Booking your lodging in advance can help you save money, as it does with many locations. Additionally, it provides you with the most hotel options and may make it easier for you to choose a place that fits within your budget. In peak season, particularly, last-minute prices can be exceedingly pricey (we've seen them quadruple the going rate).

Once you've decided on your travel dates and have your tickets reserved, I'd start looking at housing possibilities that fall within your budget. Making reservations in advance not only assures that you have a place to stay but also might save you money. It's never enjoyable to search for a place to stay by driving about late at night.

If you have the ability to cancel your reservation, it may still be a smart idea to reserve your lodging even if you are not yet certain of your intentions. Most accommodations let you reserve a hotel room, guesthouse, or apartment on several internet hotel websites, like Booking.com, and then cancel it if your plans change. You just need to cancel it by the deadline listed on the reservation (normally 24 hours to 1 week in advance depending on the property).

By making a reservation in advance, you can lock in the current price and guarantee a place to stay, but you still have the option of changing your mind later.

5. Take into account a camping trip

One of the cheapest forms of lodging in Iceland is camping, which also allows you to spend the night outside and beneath the stars. This is a fantastic way to see Iceland on a tight budget. We'll provide you with all the details you want to determine whether camping is the correct activity for you and how much you can anticipate spending per night.

Locating Campgrounds in Iceland

If you want to self-drive in Iceland, camping is one of the most affordable methods to get around. A minor overnight fee, which is presently set at 333 ISK (USD $2.78) for each tent or campervan, is added to the cost of a campsite, which ranges from 1,000 to 2,600 ISK (USD $8 to $20) per person/night. For usage of supplementary services like laundry, rubbish disposal, and showers, there are sometimes minimal additional expenses. So, before selecting a campsite, examine the prices to save money.

Are campground reservations required in advance? In Iceland, camping is available without previous reservations. In actuality, few campgrounds accept reservations in advance. People are rarely turned away, and there is often a lot of room (the majority are open fields).

Knowing where campsites are in advance may help you make general plans for where you will spend each night of your vacation. Most places operate on a first-come, first-served basis, so avoid arriving too late during peak hours, especially if you have special needs (e.g., a large caravan that needs water & electric hookups). It's a good idea to check in by early evening, and most campgrounds allow registration and check-in within specific hours, so it's a good idea to double-check.

Winter travelers should be aware that many Icelandic campgrounds are seasonal and are closed during the colder months. Therefore, when determining your driving itinerary, make careful to check the campgrounds' operational dates.

If you are hiring a campervan in Iceland, it is probable that your rental will include a list of suggested campgrounds and campsite details.

How to reduce camping costs in Iceland

If you're visiting Iceland between May and September and want to camp for a few nights or longer, you might want to look into the Camping Card. The card entitles you free overnight stays (in a campervan or tent) at any of the 40+ participating campsites for up to 2 adults and up to 4 children under the age of 16. Any campground may be occupied for a maximum of four days. It is good for up to 28 nights and will unquestionably save you money if you camp in Iceland for a few days or longer!

The Camping Card may be ordered online and sent to you before your trip or purchased once you are in Iceland. It is currently 21,900 ISK ($169). You may buy it everywhere around Iceland, including at a number of tourist information centers, rental vehicle and campervan companies, 10–11 grocery shops, and post offices.

Some RV and campervan rentals include a Camping Card or give customers the choice to prepay for one.

Do they have camping packages?

Yes, there are a few self-drive camping vacation packages that come with your campervan or RV rental, a recommended route, and camping necessities. This 12-day self-drive camping vacation package (available from May to September) is ideal for individuals who intend to tour the Ring Road. It includes your campervan rental, basic CDW insurance, camping supplies, a thorough travel schedule, and a detailed travel plan.

You may take a guided hiking tour that includes camping if you're interested in hiking and camping, such as this 5-day Landmannalaugar hiking tour or this 6-day guided trek that encompasses Iceland's two most well-known hiking paths. These excursions come with luggage transfers, meals, transportation to and from Reykjavik, and a tour guide.

Can I free camp in Iceland?

Except when you are wild camping (tent camping), the majority of the time, the answer is NO. It's a frequent misconception that camping and parking are free practically everywhere in Iceland, however, this is untrue. Iceland used to have quite lax regulations regarding unlawful RV and campervan parking, as well as fairly moderate guidelines for wild camping.

However, due to rising tourism and growing environmental damage caused by campers in recent years, new regulations were enacted, and unlawful camping is now more strictly monitored and policed. New legislation is intended to safeguard the environment, reduce traffic accidents, and shield private property from harm. Any camping (tent or campervan) that is not inside of an authorized campsite is now prohibited by many landowners and even by entire areas in Iceland.

Basically, you must spend the night at an approved campground if you wish to sleep in your car, campervan, RV, tent trailer, or any other type of motorized vehicle. The only exception is if the landlord expressly grants you permission to camp on their property, which is how many Icelanders are allowed to camp for nothing.

Iceland offers affordable camping, thus there is no justification for attempting to camp there illegally. Be a considerate visitor to this stunning nation.

There are still certain areas in Iceland where you may wild camp for FREE for one night at a time if you choose to practice traditional tent camping far away from roads and structures. It is a fantastic alternative for multi-day hiking journeys in uninhabited parts of Iceland, such as the Hornstrandir Nature Reserve or the central Highlands, however, it is still advised that you utilize a certified campground when one is close by.

There are many limitations and sites where camping of any type is prohibited, but there are still certain locations where you may tent camp lawfully for free.

We only advise tent camping in the summer unless you are an experienced camper with adequate cold-weather equipment because the rest of the year may be quite chilly and damp, which can lead to some really uncomfortable camping conditions. Summertime is without a doubt the finest time to go camping in Iceland.

Check out the Environmental Agency of Iceland website, which details all the regulations for overnight camping in Iceland, if you intend to camp there.

6. Examine Every Travel Option to Iceland

Even if you most likely already know how you want to get about Iceland, it is a good idea to weigh all of your possibilities. Depending on the number of people traveling with you, the season, and the number of days you have in Iceland, the least costly choice could change.

Although money is undoubtedly a key consideration, you should also think about how comfortable the trip will be, how long you will be in the nation, how much time you will have to plan, how much time you want to spend planning, and other significant aspects.

Travel options to Iceland:

Presented Tour

Embark on a tour with a guide that stops at the locations you wish to see. We'll take care of your itinerary, accommodation, attractions, and transportation with little to no planning required. Tours provide you the opportunity to have a very good understanding of all the key expenditures before you start the trip, even if they can be more expensive than doing everything yourself. This 6-day Ring Road trip and this 10-day Ring Road trip are two examples of guided excursions in Iceland. For a well-chosen list of alternatives, see this fantastic list of guided tours in Iceland.

Day-Trips

In Iceland, establishing a base in a city (or two) and then exploring from there is a common travel strategy. Either rent a car and drive yourself or arrange day trips. For instance, day journeys from Reykjavik and Akureyri allow you to see the majority of western and southern Iceland, respectively. If you're thinking about setting up a shop in the city's capital, check out a list of popular Reykjavik day tours to get a sense of what you may visit.

Own-Drive

Hire a vehicle, plan your own route, pick your own attractions, and make your own hotel reservations. Your bookings and spending are in your hands. Everything is in your hands!

Package for Self-Driving

You may reserve a self-drive package, in which your rental vehicle, accommodation, and any tours are pre-booked for you and an itinerary is suggested based on your tastes if you want the independence of driving yourself but don't want to put a lot of effort into organizing. To get some inspiration, you may view self-drive tours on Tour Radar here and on Guide to Iceland here.

Using Public Transportation

To move about the nation, use a public bus. Unquestionably, this is among the least expensive modes of transportation in Iceland. During the summer, you can also travel using a Bus Passport.

Camping

In Iceland, camping is among the least expensive ways to spend the night, and you may either use a standard vehicle, a campervan, or public transportation to travel about.

A hitchhiker

Although it's a common suggestion in forums and travel manuals for travelers on a budget, we don't advise using hitchhiking as your main mode of transportation in Iceland. Icelanders with whom we spoke find it weird (and dangerous) for visitors to arrive in a new nation with the intention of hitchhiking their way about. It's not the greatest (or most effective) method to get about Iceland if you just have a short amount of time to rely on the goodwill (or pity) of strangers to take you around. Instead, think about taking the bus, buying a Bus Passport, sticking to one region you can explore on foot or by bike (such as Reykjavik), or thinking about carpooling.

7. Examine Using Public Transportation

Reykjavik and the surrounding region are well-served by public transit. Compared to taxis or a rental vehicle, it is a fantastic and reasonably priced option (480 ISK for each ticket) to move about the capital. There are also bus passes available if you want to take the bus frequently while visiting Reykjavik.

If you have a precise change, you may pay the bus driver in person, or you can use the Strateo phone app to pay with a credit card in advance. For individuals holding a Reykjavik City Card, the buses are free.

Visitors may ride the free municipal buses in Akureyri, the second-largest city in the north of the nation!

The public transportation system in Iceland connects all the major towns and cities for travelers. Here, you can view the public transportation system, with Strateo operating the majority of the regular bus lines. You may use a credit card to purchase tickets for the lengthy buses.

The public bus may or may not be a suitable option for you, depending on where you're going and what you're going to see. Although towns in Iceland are well linked, many tourist attractions, such as waterfalls and rural beaches, won't be close to bus stations.

8. Purchase a Bus Passport.

The fact that regular buses only connect locations that locals will visit and may not be convenient for tourists is one of their drawbacks. However, in the summer, you may buy a Bus Passport that entitles you to ride hop-on hop-off buses that travel the whole nation and stop at the most visited tourist destinations and hiking trails in Iceland.

A variety of destinations along the South Shore are covered by the South Shore bus pass, including Hverageri, Skógarfoss, Vik, Skaftafell National Park, and Jökulsárlón Glacier Lagoon.

In the summer, Trex and Thule Travel both provide specialized hiker bus tickets and services.

If you want to take the bus frequently for a few days or longer, bus passes might be a particularly cost-effective form of transportation. To determine whether it would be a good deal for your vacation, look at the routes and schedule. You may purchase the bus passports online or when you arrive in Reykjavik.

9. Go on a Group Trip

If you want to save money on the trip and are thinking about going to Iceland alone or as a couple, you might want to think about finding some travel buddies. Everything may be more affordable for groups, including cooking meals, renting apartments, renting automobiles, and taking private trips. For instance, sharing a $600 rental car with 4 people is significantly less expensive than sharing it with 2.

Perhaps you have relatives or friends that want to go to Iceland and are prepared to go with you and divide the costs? You could also want to check out travel discussion sites like this one to see if anybody else is seeking a travel partner to Iceland if you don't know anyone and are comfortable traveling with strangers. Once in Iceland, hostels are a great way to meet other budget-conscious travelers who might be interested in splitting the cost of a rental vehicle or a shopping bill.

Be aware that sometimes little is more. You will have fewer alternatives for transportation and lodging if you are traveling in a group of five or more persons. In fact, this can result in higher travel expenses per passenger.

Compare your trip possibilities if you can't find any traveling buddies. For instance, a group bus tour may appear pricey and out of your price range, but the rates often cover practically all of your essential travel costs, such as hotels, meals, transportation, a guide, and luggage transfer. When you add up all the expenditures, especially if you are traveling alone, you could find that they wind up being less expensive (or about the same price) as doing it all yourself.

10. Research rental car companies.

If you decide to hire a car and drive throughout Iceland, you may cut costs by researching car pricing, limiting the number of rental days, and being aware of your insurance alternatives. Additionally, you should take every precaution to keep your automobile from becoming damaged because auto maintenance and repairs are expensive in Iceland.

Compare the price of renting a car (with insurance) with alternative possibilities if you are unsure whether you want to do so or not (e.g., joining tours or a Bus Passport). Renting a car in Iceland is not inexpensive, and it is not always the best choice for visitors.

Compare car rental rates

To obtain the best bargain, check costs if you're considering renting a car in Iceland.

Here are several locations to look up costs and think about making reservations:

Going north

We suggest using this online marketplace because it specializes in Icelandic car rentals. The website provides a list of vehicles, SUVs, vans, and campervans from various Icelandic rental companies. Additionally, they provide you the option to select from a variety of extra insurances that are exclusive to Iceland.

Rentalcars.com

Our go-to resource for discovering rental automobiles throughout the world is this comparison website for car rentals.

SadCars

This firm, which frequently offers the lowest prices, hires out older model cars. Nevertheless, compared to other Icelandic rental vehicle providers, it has gotten less favorable client feedback. Although we haven't utilized them and can't speak from personal experience, they could be a viable solution for individuals who are on a restricted budget. Just be sure to first look at recent reviews.

NOTE: In Iceland, you must be at least 20 years old to hire a car, and many rental agencies demand that drivers be at least 23 or 25. Drivers under 25 may occasionally be charged higher rental rates.

Reserve in advance

When visiting Iceland in the summer, you shouldn't wait until the last minute to determine whether you want to hire a car. There won't be as many possibilities for you, and the prices and remaining inventory of automobiles will be determined by the car businesses. When you require a rental car for the same day, internet rates are typically more affordable than if you contact or visit a rental car service.

Fewer Days Needed for Car Rental

Reduce the number of rental days to save money by just hiring the automobile on the days you will really be using it. Are you truly going to require a car the whole time? To save money, plan your trip such that the days you don't require a car fall together.

For instance, it is simple to take a shuttle from the airport to Reykjavik, and you can easily navigate around the city's center on foot, by bike, or by public transport. If you want to embark on any full-day excursions, like a bus tour to the Highlands or a guided glacier climb, you also don't need a car.

Choose Your Auto Insurance Wisely

Let me start by saying that, as is true of most areas, Icelandic insurance is difficult, and we do not purport to fully comprehend it or provide any legal advice. To get you started, though, we'll try to provide the fundamentals.

To legally drive a car in Iceland, you must have third-party liability insurance, which is often covered by the collision damage waiver insurance that comes with your rental car or campervan. Almost many rentals include this in the price because it is a legal obligation, so make sure to check that it is.

The required third-party liability insurance as well as owner and driver accident insurance are typically included in the Basic CDW plan. It could also come with extras like security against car theft.

A typical rental car's basic CDW has a deductible that ranges from $1,500 to $3,000, so an accident might potentially cost you up to that sum. In general, paying a little bit extra will lower the deductible.

Additionally, the standard CDW coverage often NOT included by rental vehicle costs DOES NOT cover things like cracks in the windscreen, general physical damage, sand damage, wind damage, paint scratches, water damage, etc. Given the gravel roads, wind, and several novice drivers on the road, damage including windshield chips, dents, and scratches is rather typical in Iceland.

In Iceland, parts and labor are costly, and rental car companies sometimes charge significantly more for these services. A dent from someone opening their door into your car could cost you 50,000 to 200,000 ISK (USD $387 to $1,551), and a damaged door from opening it into the wind could cost you 500,000 ISK (USD $3,878). For example, a chipped windshield could cost you 75,000 to 100,000 ISK ($581 to $775) as they'll need to replace the windshield.

Of course, the choice to acquire more insurance than what is legally necessary is entirely yours, but we strongly advise purchasing coverage for at least the most common types of damage, especially if you want to keep the car for longer than a few days and/or plan to drive on any gravel roads.

In most cases, the "Super CDW" insurance option upgrade has a zero (or extremely low) deductible and covers all common types of exterior-related physical damage to the automobile, such as paint scratches, dents, chips, broken door hinges, and windscreen cracks. This is what we bought, along with theft-prevention measures. This offered us far greater peace of mind and is what we would advise the majority of tourists to do to prevent any significant unexpected charges during their vacation.

The "sand and ash protection" add-on insurance option is another popular choice. This shields your automobile from any sand or volcanic ash damage. Sandstorms can cause damage, although they are a less frequent occurrence in Iceland, particularly on the South Coast. The main harm in this situation is that the sand (or ash) will scrape and remove the paint off your automobile, and repainting a car will clearly be an extremely expensive price.

We chose not to use the "sand and ash protection" and instead took care to monitor the state of the roads and our travel options. You'll have to use your own discretion to decide whether or not you want to buy this.

As with any insurance policy, no insurance will protect you against losses brought on by unlawful driving, including off-roading, speeding, intoxicated driving, and using blocked roads. Additionally, they won't provide coverage if you engage in activities that are prohibited by your rental agreement, which in Iceland frequently entails driving on Highland F roads (some 4X4 rentals are permitted in the summer, but carefully review your contract) or fording unbridged rivers or streams. Check the rental agreement for the vehicle you have carefully.

NOTE: Although third-party liability insurance and personal accident insurance are not optional under Icelandic law, you cannot refuse them if they are included with your credit card as CDW insurance (some American credit cards provide this as a feature) or travel insurance. In most cases, it is preferable to simply accept the CDW, but you can go to your insurance provider and the firm where you rented the automobile to discuss your particular circumstance.

Check traffic and road conditions often
The weather in Iceland may change fast and is sometimes rather unexpected, so anybody traveling there should regularly check the road conditions. Avoiding inclement weather and hazardous driving conditions can not only help you stay safe while driving, but it will also help you avoid doing expensive damage to your rental.

The two websites listed below are ones you should keep an eye on when traveling:

- Safetravel.is

Iceland Association for Search and Rescue's safety webpage

- Road.is

Webpage for current road conditions run by the Icelandic Road and Coastal Administration
These websites will provide information about closed roads, storm warnings, sandstorm alerts, high wind warnings, flood warnings, avalanche warnings, etc.

11. Think about carpooling

If you're visiting Iceland on a tight budget, a bus trip with a guide or a rental vehicle could be too pricey. Joining someone searching for passengers to split the cost or giving a lift to someone else are two ways to cut costs. On the website Samferda, you may locate a fellow traveler to join you in carpooling if you don't have the money to rent a car yourself.

If you don't have a car but want to join a carpool, you may use the straightforward website to request a ride or other passengers who are traveling to the same location in Iceland (you have a car, but want passengers to join you). Make sure that the expectations for cost-sharing are stated clearly upfront.

If you discover acceptable traveling partners who have similar destinations in mind, you may use this for a single travel requirement (like going to the airport) or even for your whole trip. This is a sensible substitute for hitchhiking.

12. Pack carefully to prevent impulse buys

Along with making sure you are prepared for your vacation, packing everything you need may also help you save money. It also pays to have the appropriate safety equipment (such as a dry bag or waterproof cover) to shield costly things (such as cameras and phones) from harm. We saw this personally as waterfall spray harmed the WIFI capabilities of our camera.

Although it is expensive, it is simple to get high-quality apparel and winter equipment in Iceland. For instance, when I looked at the cost of a basic knitted hat at a variety of shops, I struggled to find anything for less than USD $55 (a comparable hat would cost roughly USD $15 in the United States). In Iceland, prices for various consumer products, such as water bottles, towels, gadgets, camping supplies, etc., are significantly more than in most other nations.

To determine what you'll need for your vacation, it is advisable to conduct some study in advance. Then I'd advise drafting a list to ensure you bring everything you'll need in order to prevent having to buy it in Iceland. In Iceland, we encountered numerous people who arrived unprepared and had to buy warmer clothes, waterproof shoes, or appropriate hiking equipment there.

To find out what to expect from the weather, check the weather prediction both in advance and just before you go. Check out some suggested packing lists for the season you plan to go, like this Iceland winter packing list.

Check the requirements for any activities you plan to engage in while in Iceland, such as hot spas, golf, skiing, birding, and snorkeling. If you already possess items like binoculars, gloves, swimsuits, trekking poles, or ski goggles, you definitely don't want to have to rent or buy them.

Whatever the season, pack warm layers of clothes (at least a few wool items are recommended), waterproof hiking boots or shoes, windproof and waterproof outer layers, a cap, sunscreen, a swimsuit (for spas and pools), and a warm coat or jacket. You'll need thick clothes because temperatures can be chilly even in the summer.

Most vacationers also advise bringing a towel. A standard beach towel and a similar fast-drying travel towel were among the 2 towels we brought on our most recent vacation. Anyone wishing to visit the geothermal pools will benefit from bringing their own towel because it will prevent them from having to hire one, and many of the pools don't have towel rentals. A towel is useful to use to dry off if you get wet in the rain or by the spray from a waterfall when camping or staying at a hostel.

For your phone and other valuables, we advise bringing a dry bag or waterproof case, especially if you want to visit swimming pools, go on long treks, take boat trips, or engage in water sports. We advise buying a cheap rain sleeve to safeguard valuable cameras for individuals who own them. Additionally, hikers and backpackers should make sure their packs are waterproof. These things will also aid in shielding your belongings from rainstorms and waterfall spray (some waterfall spray may quickly immerse you if it's windy!).

Be extra prepared for the rain, snow, wind, and cooler weather if you're going during the winter season, which usually runs from November to the end of April. To aid with advice and suggestions, we offer a winter packing list for Iceland.

Although you won't often require full winter clothing throughout the summer (approximately from June to the end of August), it can still get cold and it never gets hot here. In order to be ready for probable cold weather, rain, and high winds, check the forecast. Since it was colder and rainier than average for June when we were there, we wore wool base layers on around 60% of the days.

You should bring an eye mask and sunglasses (or a hat) during the heat.

We strongly advise investing in a comfortable sleeping mask since the midnight sun (where the sun just briefly sets) can make it difficult to get a good night's sleep. There are a lot of hotels, inns, and flats that don't have the required blackout curtains or blinds. In order to help seal gaps in curtains and drapes, we also provided a drape clip (a few clothespins would do).

13. Look for less expensive options when eating out.

Although I wouldn't classify any of the restaurants we visited in Iceland as "affordable," there are undoubtedly some locations where you can eat while still saving money. An appetizer and the main meal for supper for one person in a typical Icelandic restaurant will cost about 6,500 ISK (about $50 USD) without beverages.

The cheapest meals in Iceland are often available in grocery shops (such as pre-made sandwiches, wraps, salads, and snack foods), fast food restaurants like Subway (only accessible in major cities and towns like Reykjavik, Akureyri, and Egilsstadir), neighborhood eateries, and gas station restaurants. There are cafes and restaurants at many museums and sites, and they frequently include moderately priced alternatives such as sandwiches, soups, waffles, and cakes.

In Iceland, a lot of individuals unwittingly adopt a soup and bread diet. Typically costing between 1,200 and 1,800 ISK, soup is the least-priced item on menus and provides a pretty nutritious choice. You frequently receive a free refill of soup, sometimes even an endless supply. According to our experience, fish soup, lamb soup, and mushroom soup are popular soup choices in Iceland.

Iceland's capital city of Reykjavik is perhaps the greatest area to obtain cheap meals. Along with grocery stores and quick food restaurants, hot dog and sandwich stalls also sell affordable meals. Popular hot dog vendor Baejarins has been selling dogs since 1937. An Icelandic hot dog costs between 400 and 500 ISK. Another widely available, reasonably priced food item is waffles.

IKEA is another spot to enjoy a cheap dinner close to Reykjavik if you have a car. Unbelievable as it may seem, Icelanders enjoy eating in the restaurant inside of this huge Swedish budget home furnishings store because of the reasonably low costs for food and alcoholic beverages. Due to the reasonable prices of the kids' meals, it is especially well-liked by individuals who have families. In fact, we went to get a towel on our first visit and ended up eating here. We were shocked by how crowded it was!

The finest locations for less costly hot meals in Iceland are actually petrol stations, making them ideal for travelers. In Iceland, there are a lot of gas stations (like the Olis and N1 chains) that sell both quick-service food (pre-made sandwiches, snacks, and drinks) and dining establishments that provide hot meals including hamburgers, hot dogs, pizza, fish stew, and paninis. A heated lunch costs between 1,500 and 2,500 ISK.

Based on our personal experience, the cuisine at different gas stations ranges from very decent to subpar, however, these locations often have the greatest rates in town. Keep in mind that not all gas stations provide dining options or retail establishments, particularly those in more isolated locations, which may only have a collection of mechanical gas pumps.

Just be aware that even at well-known retailers like Subway or IKEA, pricing will be greater than you are accustomed to. For instance, a Subway sandwich will cost you around twice as much in Iceland as it would in the United States, yet it still represents a great value given Icelandic restaurant rates!

If you're attempting to make a food budget, you could definitely get by on as little as $20 per person per day, but it would take a lot of effort! If your budget is really tight, you'll probably have to prepare your own meals, split meals with someone else, or settle for a few and/or other alternatives.

A more reasonable budget would be $50 per person per day for three meals each day. However, even at $50 per person per day, you will still have certain restrictions, particularly if you want to dine at sit-down restaurants. So, how and where you choose to go and eat will actually determine your budget.

14. Prepare Your Own Food

You have the choice to prepare your own meals if you reserve self-catering accommodation or a campground. Even though groceries in Iceland are more costly than in most other parts of Europe (a loaf of bread cost USD $4 when we were there last), cooking your own meals instead of eating out may still save you money.

Shopping at food stores with cheaper prices, where the same things may be found for up to 50% less than in other stores, will help you save money in Iceland, as it does in most other nations. We advise visiting the low-cost grocery store chains Bónus, Nettó, and Kronan while in Iceland. Budget customers are advised to stay away from the 10–11 convenience stores since they are, on average, significantly more costly than other grocery stores in Iceland.

The majority of supermarkets, including the three low-cost supermarkets mentioned above, feature a budget brand for necessities. Keep an eye out for these products because they are frequently the most affordable choice in that category (e.g., the least coffee, or paper towels). For instance, Euro Shopper is the low-cost brand in Bónus, whereas Coop and X-tra items are available through Nettó.

If you plan to do a lot of grocery shopping while visiting Iceland, you may save some money by taking a few reusable bags because supermarket bags are not free and plastic bags cannot be sold to consumers. Alternatively, you may buy reusable bags from food shops.

How to Locate Self-Catering Accommodation

There are several self-catering choices available, including hostels, flats, and campsites designed for people who like to prepare their own meals. The majority of hotels, guesthouses, and B&Bs forbid visitors from doing their own cooking.

If you are traveling for a longer period of time, staying in an apartment, hostel, or camping that also offers laundry services might allow you to avoid paying for hotel laundry services. For information on how to do and save money on laundry while traveling, see our guide.

Here are some excellent starting points for your search:

Residences -

In Iceland, the majority of flats include a kitchen and some basic kitchenware.

Pensions -

The majority of hostels in Iceland provide communal kitchens where guests may prepare their own meals.

Vrbo –

Many of the accommodations on Vrbo have a kitchen where you may prepare your own meals. To make sure you can cook, check the house rules before making a reservation.

Campgrounds -

If you have your own camping stove, you can prepare simple meals, and some campgrounds provide communal cooking facilities.

15. Drink in moderation

Alcohol is quite costly in Iceland, whether you buy it at a shop or order a drink in a bar or restaurant, due to high taxes and import costs. Alcohol costs in Iceland are now among the highest in the world.

The greatest approach to saving money is to abstain from drinking, but if you are unable to do so, you might attempt to find the least expensive drinking establishments.

First off, the duty-free section of the airport generally has the cheapest booze. Consider purchasing alcohol either at the airport where you are departing (if permitted) or at the Keflavik International Airport when you get there. The least priced and most practical alternative is likely to be the duty-free store at Keflavik for the majority of travelers.

Individual drinks in a bar are frequently more expensive than buying a complete bottle of liquor or a 6-pack of beer. However, there are certain restrictions on where you may buy alcohol in Iceland, and you are not allowed to buy alcohol at supermarkets or gas stations. Only the duty-free shop at the airport and the state-run outlets known as Vinbudin sell alcohol in Iceland. In Iceland, you must be at least 20 years old to buy alcohol.

If you want to go out, look for happy hours where you can get 2 for 1 or cheaper drinks. We discovered that during happy hours, beverages can be discounted by up to 50%.

You should be aware that the majority of happy hour deals are only available in bigger towns and cities like Reykjavik (check out the Appy Hour app from your Appstore or Play Store) and Akureyri, so it could be difficult to locate cheaper beverages in smaller towns or rural regions.

Iceland has highly strong regulations against drinking and driving, and even very low blood alcohol levels might result in arrest. Drunk driving is seen as a serious crime, and fines are highly steep (even for first-time offenders). So be sure to hold off on drinking until you have finished your nighttime journey!

16. Sip bottled water

Icelandic beverages are pricey, but the country's tap water is free and safe to drink. Iceland's drinking water is of exceptionally good quality. Simply inquire if you are unclear whether the water is safe to drink somewhere.

Pitchers of water are frequently available for customers to help themselves from in cafes, gas stations, and fast food restaurants. In sit-down restaurants, pitchers of water are also frequently given to the table. If not, simply ask for water when placing an order.

Bring a reusable water bottle with you to avoid paying for beverages or buying bottled water by filling it up at water fountains and sinks. We personally like these two water bottles if you need to get one for your journey. You'll spend less money and produce less plastic garbage as a result.

NOTE: Because geothermal water in some parts of Iceland, particularly Reykjavik, is pumped up directly from the earth, it tastes and smells sulfurous. Although it tastes bad and isn't meant to be consumed, it is safe to drink. Cold water, on the other hand, comes from a separate source and is pure and safe to drink. So before filling your bottle, simply let the water flow cold.

17. Make use of fuel coupons

Fuel discount cards might help you save a little money on fuel and gas station purchases if you drive.

If your city or town has several gas stations, you may compare rates to see which ones are most affordable. Although there are additional names including Shell, Skeljungur, and Orkan, Olis and N1 were the two most prevalent brands we encountered in Iceland. In actuality, though, you're lucky to locate more than one station in less populated locations because there are frequently few options available.

Nevertheless, obtaining a discount card from one (or more) of the gasoline networks is one option to save money. As far as we are aware (as of May 2022), Iceland offers discount cards from both Olis and Orkan/Skeljungur. If you are renting a car or campervan, there is a considerable likelihood that your keys may include a discount card or key fob.

On both of our trips to Iceland, the vehicle rental business had an Olis discount card linked to our key fob. However, you can also get an Olis discount card at the gas stations. We received discounts of up to 10% off at the restaurant as well as a 3% discount on petrol. The discount is available on nearly everything in the convenience store, which frequently stocks a variety of items including meals, snacks, auto accessories, basic groceries, souvenirs, and travel-related items (maps, guidebooks). Some goods, including cigarettes, are NOT eligible for the discount.

A credit card with a four-digit pin is required since many petrol stations in smaller towns are unattended after regular work hours. You can obtain prepaid cards that will function at the pumps if you don't have a credit card or a PIN set up (recommend doing this before your trip). An example of one of these cards is the N1 card.

18. Look for Free Activities

There are a lot of free things to do in Iceland, despite the fact that many of the attractions, excursions, and museums might be pricey.

Here are some suggestions for affordable and free activities in Iceland:

Many of Iceland's most well-known sites, including geysers, waterfalls, beaches, parks, public art projects, churches, and lava fields, are free to explore. It is simple to plan a trip that includes a lot of free attractions.
There are a ton of free activities in Reykjavik. A few options include taking a "free" walking tour

(donations are appreciated), admiring the Hallgrmskirkja (free to visit, though there is a small fee to climb the church tower), sampling the cuisine at the Hlemmur Food Hall, visiting the botanic garden, hiking through the "skjuhl," or perusing the weekend Kolaportid flea market.
Make time for outdoor pursuits like hiking, swimming, skiing, scenic drives, looking for the Northern Lights, birding, climbing, riding, or picnics that are either free or affordable.

Utilize all the advantages your hotel has to offer. Sometimes it pays to book a room at a pricier hotel. For instance, some hotels provide complimentary access to their on-site hot tub and spa, swimming pools, bird-watching binoculars, and free bike and canoe rentals.

Visiting a hot pool in Iceland doesn't cost much if anything at all. For instance, the Nauthólsvk beach and hot pool in Reykjavik are free throughout the summer, and you may locate little hot pools that are either free or affordable or donation-only in less popular locations of Iceland (e.g., Westfjords).

In practically every town in Iceland, there are public city pools that are free to use and a terrific location to socialize.

Check to see if there are any free museum days, festivals, concerts, or other activities going on while you're away. In places like Reykjavik and Akureyri, there is nearly always something free going on, especially on the weekends during the summer!

Iceland's outdoor pools are either free or reasonably priced.

19. Use coupons and discounted passes to your advantage

Searching for discount passes, deals, and coupons that are accessible might help you save money at numerous places. We've included a few of the ones we're aware of below, but we advise keeping an eye out for offers as you travel. For instance, many attractions provide visitors who buy ticket discounts to other neighboring attractions.

Consider these discount cards and discounts for Iceland:

Iceland City Card

The Reykjavik City Card grants free admission to a number of museums and attractions in Reykjavik, including the National Museum of Iceland, the National Gallery of Iceland, (open-air museum), and Reykjavik Zoo & Family Park. Free bus transportation throughout the city, access to the city's public hot pools and saunas, and special deals for dining establishments and tourist attractions are all included. Even though it's not intended for everyone, using the bus and planning to visit several of the included sites while in the capital will save you a lot of money. We utilized it on our first vacation and it helped us save money.

Icelandic Discounts

This paper discount booklet (which is now available as an app) offers you a number of discounts to a variety of Icelandic tourist sites and services, including restaurants, car rentals, spas, pubs, and tours. The coupon book costs just approximately 1,500 ISK and applying one coupon frequently results in a financial gain. The best aspect is that you can check the majority of coupon offers online before making a purchase to determine whether it will result in savings. Both the new app and the Icelandic coupon book are available for purchase there.

Icelandic Art Museum

This is not a pass, but as there are three different locations of the museum in the city, if you pay for entrance to one, you also get free access to the other two. The entrance pass is good for access to Hafnarhus, Kjarvalsstair, and the Asmundur Sveinsson Sculpture Museum for 24 hours. m. A solid buy for art enthusiasts.

Camping Permit.

Anyone wishing to camp in Iceland should take into consideration the card that was previously stated under the camping part. The card entitles up to 2 people and up to 4 children under the age of 16 to stay in any of the 40+ participating campsites for a maximum of 28 nights in a tent or campervan! Each campground only allows overnight stays of up to 4 nights.

Membership in Hostelling International

Consider joining this non-profit hosteling group if your primary lodging preference is in hostels. Members of the Hosteling International network, which includes many hostels throughout Iceland and across the world, receive discounts of at least 10% off regular rates. A cheap 12-month subscription may be purchased at any participating hostel or in advance online.

20. Invest Money in Experiences & Tours You'll Remember

If you have a limited budget and are visiting Iceland, you should invest it in memorable experiences. Fortunately, Iceland has a ton of free activities to enjoy! However, we advise all visitors to Iceland, even those on a tight budget, to pick one or two particular items to indulge in while there.

For many, visiting the Blue Lagoon is a must-do luxury experience. For others, though, it may be a glacier trek, tectonic plate diving, reindeer safari, whale & puffin boat trip, Northern Lights Jeep hunting tour, beer walking tour, or ice cave exploration.

Another option is to spend the day visiting the museums in Reykjavik, attend a show at the Harpa in the evening, spend the night in a "space pod" at the Galaxy Pod Hostel, or go out to a nice meal.

Your options should be determined by your hobbies and budget. Just pick activities that you believe will be worthwhile and stick them in your memory after the vacation!

21. Be Ready!

Finally, we just want to stress how important it is to plan ahead and do some study before your trip. Because they didn't do any study before their trip, consumers frequently wind up paying more than they anticipated. Particularly in an expensive place like Iceland, those who go there unprepared are far more likely to end up spending more money.

Budget travelers visiting Iceland don't necessarily need to plan out every day of their vacation, but they should at least conduct some research. Read up on Iceland's culture and history, decide which locations you must see, become familiar with exchange rates and typical prices, reserve essentials like tours in advance, monitor weather predictions and road conditions, and pack essentials like rain gear, warm clothes, and swimsuits. You may travel more wisely and save money in Iceland by planning ahead a little.

CHAPTER 5

Information About Safety In Iceland For Visitors

Iceland may differ slightly from other well-known holiday spots you visit due to its subarctic temperature and little population. Mountains, waterfalls, geothermal places, deserted locations, and the ocean are examples of natural wonders that are not only stunning but also take you by surprise if you are not prepared. Use these eight safety recommendations to your advantage when you organize your vacation to Iceland.

Be familiar with Iceland's 911 digits

First and foremost, dial Iceland's emergency hotline if you're in trouble and need assistance right away. The emergency number is 112. This number is the same as in many other nations. You may call it for free to get in touch with the police, ambulances, and other emergency services. In Iceland, there are around 100 rescue teams with tens of thousands of volunteers that react to distress calls, avert accidents, and save lives. While on your trip, think about making a donation to the Icelandic Association for Search and Rescue (ICE-SAR) so they may continue their outstanding job!

Pay attention to the weather report

Extreme weather can occasionally occur in Iceland due to its variable climate. Snow and high wind gusts are prevalent during the winter and will significantly reduce visibility. So, before leaving, it's a good idea to check the weather prediction on www.vedur.is. If this means you won't be traveling through a snowstorm, you might wish to leave earlier in the day or postpone your trip for a few hours. When planning your vacation in the summer, especially if you're hiking and camping, keep in mind the high wind speeds, fog, low temperatures, and rain. Knowing the weather prediction can help you dress appropriately and plan for it, making your vacation much more pleasurable.

Before you go, check the state of the roads.

Be careful to visit www.road.is to check the road conditions as well as the weather prediction. The Icelandic Road and Coastal Administration routinely updates its webpage, indicating whether roads are blocked, slick, contain ice spots, or are straightforward to travel. Never drive on a blocked road; it might be risky and leave you stranded. Additionally, Road.is indicates if your route calls for a 4WD vehicle. Only drive across rivers if you have the right vehicle, are knowledgeable about the area, or are accompanied by an experienced driver or guide. Here is additional information about driving safely in Iceland.

When visiting geothermal zones, use special caution.

Swimming pools, spas, and natural baths in Iceland all use geothermal energy to warm the water. Residential heating systems and even Winter Street heating use geothermal energy. However, geothermal energy is not just practical; geothermal regions, with their sulfurous mud pools, hot springs, and steaming fumaroles, are also well-liked tourist destinations. You might be surprised to learn that the water in these mud pools can become as hot as 100°C. It is exceedingly risky to deviate from the path in certain sections since you might suffer severe burns if you fall in or even slide in with your foot. Fortunately, there are clear pathways across these locations, so be careful to follow them.

Avoid getting too near to the water.

Sneaker waves, have you ever heard of them? If not, you should research them before visiting Iceland. Sneaker waves, also known as sleeper waves, are waves that extend far farther out onto the coast than typical waves and surprise unsuspecting shore residents. Some of these waves are so large that they violently pull individuals into the water. Reynisfjara and Kirkjufjara beaches in South Iceland frequently experience sneaker waves, and warning signs have been installed as a result of several sneaker wave-related fatalities in recent years. It's okay to travel to these places as long as you keep your distance from the sea and keep in mind that you cannot dip your toes in the ocean there.

Keep along the route.

It's crucial to keep on the route when visiting any natural marvel, whether it's a waterfall, geothermal region, mountain walk, or other location. This will not only conserve nature, but it will also allow you to enjoy it in the safest possible manner. It occasionally happens that regions are restricted to protect the environment or because a way is dangerous. Do not cross the line if you observe a closed path. It is shut down for a cause. You should be alright as long as you obey road and path restrictions.

Let someone know your destination.

The next rule is particularly crucial if you're going to go hiking, camping, or hitchhiking, but anybody leaving the city can post their trip itinerary on www.safetravel.is, the website of SafeTravel, an ICE-SAR project dedicated to accident prevention. You must provide at least one place every day for this, but the more details the better. They also request information about an emergency contact and you. In case your last-minute plans change, be sure to provide an updated travel itinerary. If ICE-

SAR is aware of your travel itinerary, they will be able to act more quickly in an emergency.

Stay up to date with safetravel.is

Although SafeTravel was stated in the sentence before this one, you should also utilize its website while you're there to look up any safety advisories. It is a fantastic resource for tourists visiting Iceland.

SafeTravel attempts to inform and enlighten travelers by offering resources. Daily updates to their website's safety alerts are made in English, German, French, and Icelandic. If you wish to speak with a safety agent in person, you can do so at the What's On visitor center at Bankastraeti 2 or by Skype from 8:00 am to 10:00 pm every day.

Strange Icelandic Traditions, Customs, and Habits You Might Not Expect

The modern Icelander is a fashionable, technologically aware, and knowledgeable individual. The connections to antiquated customs and beliefs are yet strong.

Many things that are commonplace in Iceland may seem weird to someone from outside the country. Therefore, we've compiled a list of Icelandic customs and habits to help you be ready for your vacation there.

Þorrablót

The celebration of shark fins, harsh whiskey, and ram testicles
Despite having a more laid-back culture, Iceland has many strictly adhered-to customs, particularly when it comes to cuisine. The Þorrablót (Thorrablót) is the most well-known of them. In

Iceland, January and February are dedicated to commemorating the ancient Norse month of Porri.

Families and sometimes whole counties gather around this time to consume traditional foods like fermented shark, pickled ram's testicles, and boiling sheep's heads.

Fortunately, Icelandic food preservation techniques have advanced, so we no longer need to pickle or ferment our food to keep it fresh. But Porrablót is a great way to visit with loved ones, honor the customs of the past, and remember our forefathers.

The three-day extravagant food festival in Iceland

Each year, Icelanders observe Bolludagur (Bun Day), Sprengidagur (Shrove Tuesday), and in late February or early March (Ash Wednesday). Instead of Ash Wednesday signaling the beginning of Lent, in Iceland it signifies the conclusion of a three-day feast during which Icelanders consume an abundance of both sweet and savory treats.

On Bun Day, kids craft customary wands that they use to swat their parents into feeding them delicious, chocolate buns. There are a lot of hurting adult behinds when you have one bun for every slap.

To balance off all the sweetness from the previous day, Bolludagur Iceland Shrove Tuesday (more accurately, "Eat-Till-You-Burst Day") provides a ton of salty beef and peas.

Ash Wednesday, a sort of Icelandic Halloween, comes in third and last. Children enter stores dressed as characters and sing for sweets. It turns out that our kids are quite disciplined, especially when it comes to sugar.

Making little pouches and secretly hanging them on people's backs without their knowledge is another ritual. Even yet, it happens less frequently every year.

Sheep gatherings

For farmers and sheep aficionados alike, September and October are exciting months because that's when the sheep round-ups happen.

Summertime sees Icelandic sheep grazing freely. They are sheep, not migratory birds, thus they do not understand when to migrate to warmer climates (i.e. the barn). Therefore, someone needs to go fetch them, which is where round-ups come in.

Farmers gather all the local sheep into designated corrals with the help of neighbors, relatives, or random strangers.

Since sheep are creatures of habit and every farmer is aware of where their particular flock likes to congregate, most of them can typically be found quite quickly. Each farmer goes in search of his sheep as the sorting process starts once all the sheep are secure in the corrals.

People cheer each other on and typically pass around a flask of some sort of alcoholic courage throughout this exciting occasion. After the sheep have all been safely placed, an evening ball is thrown where folks may celebrate a job well done and use that liquid bravery to more amorous uses.

Namesakes from Iceland

Let's use an illustration.

The offspring of our new hypothetical marriage Einar Gunnarsson and Sigrn Felixdóttir are Gunnar, a male, and Ingibjörg, a girl. Then Gunnar Einarsson and Ingibjörg Einarsdóttir are those kids (the son and daughter of Einar).

Then Gunnar had a son, whom he named Einar in honor of his father. Then, Einar Gunnarsson, who is what we refer to as "alnafni," or "full namesake," was born. However, Einar Ingibjargarson is "just" a nafni (a namesake) and not an alnafni if Ingibjörg and her husband have a son and name him Einar Ingibjargarson.

The amusing part about this is that when you share a name with someone else, we use these terms A LOT. You frequently say "hi namesake" when you greet someone, even though they are absolutely unrelated to you.

Nafni and Nafna are the masculine and female equivalents, respectively.

Icelanders get six months to decide on a child's name.

Time is a factor in yet another name custom that appears peculiar. The naming of children is not a priority for Icelanders. People throughout the world use their given names to announce the birth of their offspring. "Our girl was born this morning, she weighed 3,829 grams, and she was 49 cm tall. Everyone is healthy and doing fantastic," will be all that is said in Iceland.

The christening or naming ceremony is when the name is revealed (for those less religious). This ritual, though, might take place months after the infant is born. Many Icelanders are said to have nicknames that have nothing to do with their real names, according to others. Simply something that remained in place while we waited for their "true" name.

Icelandic parents are legally given six months to register the name of their child. On the contrary, if they wait any longer, they will be penalized (about ISK 1,500 a day).

Icelandic weather superstitions

Perhaps unsurprisingly, the weather has a significant impact on Icelanders' daily life. It is an untamed, capricious beast with a strong anger that it is not hesitant to display. Icelanders have nonetheless done their best throughout the years to comprehend her and avoid offending her.

Numerous traditions and customs have emerged as a result of these efforts. You should never walk on a blacksmith (a black beetle), for instance, as it will induce rain. Similarly, you should never leave your rake with its teeth pointing up since doing so will also cause rain.

Another significant factor in our superstition is dreams. The likelihood that it will snow for the same number of days as the white sheep increases if you see them in your dreams.

Additionally, the phrase "Red sky at night, sailor's joy" is used in Iceland. Sailing warning: red sky in the morning. However, it is written Kvöldroðinn bætir og segir satt. Morgan Roinn and murat. This translates roughly to "Redness at night improves and speaks the truth." Morning redness dampens and irritates the hat. Icelandic proverbs may have a delightful quality while being utterly impolite.

Superstitions regarding dwellings in Iceland

Different superstitions are widespread in Iceland, to the point where actions associated with them have become customary. Bring bread and salt first when moving into a new home so that there will never be a food shortage. But resist any attempts to hand you a knife. Even though they cost just ISK 1, knives must always be purchased to avoid damaging your friendship with the donor and bringing ill luck.

The craft of casting curses

That does exist in Iceland, indeed. Many things may be thought of as being unlucky, yet there are workarounds. In many nations, knocking on wood is a customary practice to avoid tempting fate, but in Iceland, you also need to speak the numbers 7, 9, and 13 aloud. By pronouncing these numerals, which are said to have a particular power, you are doubly shielded from the capricious whims of fate. Therefore breaking the spell you just cast.

I'm the only one who hasn't been sick with the flu, for instance. You immediately run to bang on actual wood while repeating 7, 9, and 13 after realizing you've just put a small curse on yourself. Suddenly, the spell is broken!

Icelandic romantic superstitions

If someone gives you a piece of licorice candy called "pal" be sure to accept two pieces unless you want to spend the rest of your life alone. It is undeniably wonderful.

Winning at cards may also spell bad luck in relationships, or at least that's what you tell your opponent after they defeat you in a game. "Lucky in cards, unfortunate in love," we say.

The third is that if you don't look people in the eye when you raise your glass to toast your fellow diners, your love life will suffer. It is understandable why there are only 360,000 of us in the nation with all these romantic dangers.

How to cope with boogers in Iceland

There's a good possibility you'll get a cold or two in your life if you reside in a nation known for ice. But unlike most countries, Icelanders don't deal with boogers in the same manner. No, especially not in front of other people, do we blow our nostrils. In fact, we think it's rather disrespectful.

However, we found that merely sucking the boogers backup is OK. Before ultimately going into the restroom and blowing our nostrils privately, we will repeat this process around 100 times. It seems like something that should be kept secret, out of earshot, and out of sight. Knowing this will cause you to pay attention.

Thanks for the final time

Icelanders are incredibly kind and cordial. While it is usual everywhere to express gratitude to others for food or favors rendered, Icelanders also express gratitude to one another for time spent together, particularly when it was for a special event. Therefore, if you run into someone you were with at a recent wedding or birthday celebration, be sure to say "thanks for last time" or "takk fyrir sast" to them.

Constantly discussing the weather

If you ever find yourself in an awkward discussion with an Icelander, just change the subject to the weather, and the awkwardness is instantly over.

We like discussing it in all weather conditions, including bright, cloudy, windy, and snowy ones. Particularly if it happens all at once. Even the weather from a few days ago or the prediction for the coming week will be discussed. As long as you let us chat about the weather in Iceland, it really doesn't matter.

Conclusion

Discover Iceland's spectacular landscapes, which include imposing waterfalls, lunar-like valleys, steep glaciers, and breathtaking volcanoes, and bask in its unmatched natural beauty. Along with enjoying the local cuisine, you may participate in the lively Nordic island customs.

Made in the USA
Thornton, CO
08/01/23 19:39:28